Cuisine for Whole Health

Cuisine for Whole Health

Recipes for a Sustainable Life

Pauli Halstead

Hood River Press
Hood River, Oregon

Hood River Press
Hood River, Oregon
www.cuisineforwholehealth.com

Copyright © 2009 by Pauli Halstead
All rights reserved. Published 2009
Printed in the United States of America

ISBN 978-0-615-29959-4
Library of Congress Control Number 2009933851

Cover design by Patrick Dougherty and Jennifer Omner
Interior design by Jennifer Omner, ALL Publications
Photos on page 10 and 49 by Michael Friend
Other photos by Pauli Halstead

For Mom and Dad

We actually have the capacity and key information that can allow us to live longer and healthier than we ever have before in our long evolutionary history . . . but only if we have the wisdom to actually use it.

—NORA GEDGAUDAS, *Primal Body—Primal Mind*

Contents

A Note to the Reader

Writing this book has been a transformative process. It has made me examine and re-examine all my beliefs about food and what food is for. I have had to let go of all previous ideas of right and wrong eating and what others are doing or not doing with their diets. If anything, the process of deciding where I stood on many issues kept collapsing as I was presented with yet another way to look at things. In this process I have been thoroughly cooked.

A question has arisen. Is it our beliefs about food that make it good or not good for us? The raw food folks (some eat raw meat) believe that their way is the best for optimum health. The vegetarians believe that a plant-based diet is the kindest to the animals that we share the planet with. The vegans support not using any animal products at all or wearing anything made from an animal. Some of the meat-eating people I know are at least switching to grass-fed meats and wild-caught fish. Everyone has experts, doctors, and scientists, with published scientific studies, to back up their point of view. So how do we distill all this information to decide what it is we want to feed ourselves? It's sort of like cutting through dietary materialism.

Some of us who are committed to creating a more sustainable social and global environment are still in a quandary about what to eat and many are still very attached to their food habits. I have noticed everyone has *very* strong opinions about what to eat.

What I am learning is that in the process of eating, when it is done consciously, the body fully absorbs the life force that is in the food. Through meditation and the conscious alignment with Divine Love, what we eat gets transmuted and the result is energetic love to be shared and made useful in the world.

Cooking food together, sharing food, and growing food are about interaction and interaction supports loving. I believe it is the combined sharing of food, and all that it entails, that nourishes us. Divine Love is the sustenance we have been craving all of our lives and the reason we overeat when it's not present. We are looking for love and nourishment in what we eat. When we turn our attention to God in gratitude and love, His Love comes pouring back into our bodies, blessing us and sustaining us. We are actually digesting Divine Love and absorbing it into the very cells and bones in our body. This is the true sustenance with which the body thrives.

Our part is to listen to our bodies, which requires deep inquiry, to find out what our body is really asking for, and this might be different for each person. This is obviously not a one size fits all approach and respect must be given to whatever choice someone has made. There is no right and wrong, but there is inquiry and dialogue, dialogue with your body and dialogue with others. There will be modifications and changes as we go along. Eating *sustainably* is eating just what your body requires in that moment so that the nourishment will carry you and support you in living a life of usefulness. Our gratitude allows us to love God in all things, our food, our planet, ourselves and in each other.

Pauli and Elle

Acknowledgements

I would like to thank my Santa Fe friend, Barbara Roth who helped me edit a portion of the recipes. Her eagle eye and wonderful suggestions helped me immensely. Nora Gedgaudas, author of *Primal Body—Primal Mind*, has been extremely generous in allowing me to quote her extensively for this book. Letting go of a lifetime of sugar addiction is no small thing and Nora has been able to help me with her vast knowledge of how the body functions and the nutritional support it needs, but more importantly her compassion and her desire to help me achieve optimal health. She is truly a cheerleader and buddy.

Dr. Diana Schwarzbein, author of *The Schwarzbein Principle* and Dr. Mark Hyman, author of *The UltraMind Solution*, were also very generous in allowing me to quote them. They are helping to bring into public awareness the importance of diet and its relation to our physical and mental health. It is apparent that only we, as individuals, can affect our health by what we choose to eat. We can no longer depend on our government or our overburdened health care system to help us and we can no longer ignore the current facts these health care practitioners and many others have made public. Our very lives and the health of our planet depend on it.

My dear friend Lei accompanied me on all the trips to the Portland and Beaverton Farmer's Market. Lei carried my bags and camera, not to mention all the produce. I actually left my good camera at one of the stalls only to realize later it was missing, with all the photos I had taken. It wasn't the camera I was worried about but all those photos. We backtracked and fortunately it was still on the table where I left it. Lei and I spent many happy hours looking at all the gorgeous Oregon produce and tasting all the delicious offerings of the vendors. It was so inspiring to see all the people who come to these farmer's markets every week with their families to enjoy the good food, the wonderful music, the fabulous flowers and plants for sale and just hang out with the rest of humanity to enjoy the day. Thank you so much Lei for all your love that you give.

I would never have written this book if it had not been for my teacher and friend Elle Collier Re who has been an inspiration and a guiding support during the three years since our meeting in Santa Fe. I came to live with Elle in Hood River, at HeartGate Sanctuary, two years ago in March, to learn the art of forgiveness and unconditional love from this remarkable teacher. She has helped me let go of the past and learn to live in the eternal now presence of love. Elle's teaching is simple: every day is a blessing and an opportunity to love everyone we meet with no exceptions.

All those who come to HeartGate have also been encouraging of my efforts to write the book and have greatly appreciated the recipe testing, especially the Coconut Bliss Truffles, which are now a constant in the refrigerator. Michael, Elle's husband of twenty years, has helped me with the photos and is always fixing my computer conundrums as I am amongst those who are electronically impaired. My longtime friend Bill Austin gave me his camera to take the photos and also the beautiful Japanese knife which I use every day with pleasure. Bill has always encouraged me to accomplish more and have confidence in my abilities.

I would like to acknowledge my family, which includes my three brothers, Bob, Glenn, and Chuck and three children, John, Shannon, and Devon and one grandchild, Michael. We have all had our health issues in recent years and all of the research for the book has been for a purpose, to be able to understand the past, so we can make our present the most positive possible.

My goal in writing this book is to create enthusiasm and interest with the recipes so that achieving greater health for ourselves and our families is something that brings joy into daily life.

A Word About the Sustainable Life Diet

It's not going to be fun unless it's delicious. Period! What if everything you needed to make the change to sustainable healthy eating was fun and delicious? The reason most eating plans don't work is they are *boring* and you feel like you're being punished. You can hardly wait until your designated time frame is up and you can return to your old habits. Sustainability is one of the buzzwords of our age, but do we include our body as something we consider sustaining? Probably not! We are all hoping we can keep going no matter what we feed ourselves. Our bodies are now screaming at us in a number of different ways. Enough already!

Are you ready to take *complete responsibility* for feeling well both mentally and physically? If the answer is no you can quit reading right now. If you're saying, "Yes," there's hope and help. Diets don't work, this has been proven. Have you ever started a diet and had your energy crash and then become so totally obsessed with food you couldn't think straight? Sounds familiar doesn't it? So what will work? What *will* work is what your body will respond to, energetically, from the food you eat. If you are suffering from low energy and general malaise that might just be a clue. You wouldn't put bad motor oil in your car, so why put foods in your body that yield a low energy result, or worse, cause you to get sick? Your body has gone to sleep on you in certain ways. If you feed your body the right foods, however, it has the ability to rebalance, heal and sustain your precious life.

Having had a lot of bad eating habits over a lifetime, and the resulting illnesses, depression, anxieties and just not feeling totally up to par, I finally decided to take responsibility for what I was eating. I've been a chef and caterer for over thirty years, and even though I was cooking fabulous wine-country cuisine, my body and brain began deserting me in a number of ways. I had to make a change. It wasn't easy and it took some perseverance but it has been well worth it. Now I have both, wonderful cuisine and a healthy body. The two are mutually *inclusive* after all.

If you have some health problems, anxiety, depression or even a more serious disease, like celiac disease (an allergy to gluten), the root cause may be a systemic imbalance in your body. You may need to be under a doctor's care if it's very serious. It is now scientifically proven that almost all diseases, both mental and physical, such as diabetes, obesity, Alzheimer's, chronic fatigue syndrome, ADHD, bi-polar disorder, and various other depressions are the result of poor assimilation of food, food allergies, heavy metal toxicity, environmental toxins, and digestive imbalances. Many of the diseases affecting Americans today can be cured or greatly alleviated by a change in diet, supplementing with vitamins and minerals, drinking pure filtered water and detoxifying from heavy metals, yeast overgrowth, and various molds. By making significant dietary changes our dependence on pharmaceuticals and over the counter medications will be greatly reduced and even eliminated. As a result our medical bills will also decrease. Poor diets equal disease and increased medical expenses. It's as simple as that. Just imagine what it will be like to live a life where you feel good all the time. *It is possible.*

All humans have the same evolutionary genetics; no matter what blood type they happen to have, so there are basic foods that have worked from prehistoric times to help us evolve. Contemporary humans have been on earth for about 200,000 years and during that time we have survived and thrived without the need for processed foods, medical interventions or pharmaceuticals. These natural foods are wild-caught fish and grass-fed game (high in omega-3 fatty acids), organic vegetables, nuts, seeds, and berries. These are the foods our ancestors ate before cultivation of grains began about 10,000 years ago. Our bodies and our brains developed on these nutrient dense foods.

At no previous time in history has man eaten the foods that are now prevalent in the American diet. The American food pyramid is a joke. Only since the industrial revolution has whole food nutrition been replaced by junk processed foods, genetically modified plants, and hormone and antibiotic supplemented animals. We are eating too many empty calories and the chemicals and food additives, which are allowed in our food supply by the Federal Food and Drug Administration (FDA), are making us ill. We are now spending billions, even trillions, of dollars on health care without addressing the simple fact that many illnesses may be caused by our nutrient deficient diet. Now the scientific facts bear this theory out. The tests have been done and analyzed, the papers have been written and published. The foods we choose to eat (and not eat) have *everything* to do with our health.

Its time we took matters back into our own hands, and not trust the FDA to protect us when it comes to our national food supply. Trying to be heard by congress over all the food manufacturing lobbyists, commercial agribusiness interests and petrochemical fertilizer companies is going to be really slow going. Our *vote* to have unadulterated whole foods begins at the grocery store. Don't buy the bad stuff and maybe all the manufacturers and *pushers of toxic foods* will get the message. Be an activist and let them know we're mad as hell and we're not going to eat it any more.

This book was written to give you facts and information, which will help you get organized and begin a path to whole health. In choosing healthy sustainable foods you will see that these choices are also supportive of a sustainable planet and a better future for our children and the generations that come after us. We want to leave the earth in a better condition than we found it. There's work to do and each of us, by eating sustainably, will make a contribution to the success of this endeavor.

We can live a life that is symptom free and full of vibrant energy. *All things are possible.*

To Your Whole Health,
Pauli Halstead

The extension of the law of non-violence in the domain of economics means nothing less than the introduction of moral values to be used in regulating international commerce . . . you cannot build a non-violent society based on exploitation. Exploitation is the essence of violence.
—Mahatma Gandhi

César Chavez and The United Farm Workers

It would not be appropriate in writing this cookbook to overlook the contribution of César Chavez in forming The United Farm Workers Association, which he founded in 1962. Because of César's tireless leadership and non-violent tactics, which included the Delano grape strike and the 350-mile march to Sacramento in 1966 to ask the state government to permit farm workers to organize into a union and allow collective bargaining agreements, that people were made aware of the struggles of farm workers and their need for better pay and safer working conditions.

César used fasting, in the same way that Gandhi used it, to bring home the point that the suffering of the farm workers and their children from poverty, lack of decent housing, and the dangers of pesticides must come to an end. César saw the fast as a declaration of non-cooperation with supermarkets who promote and sell and profit from "pesticide sprayed" California table grapes.

Unfortunately the struggle goes on today here at home and in countries around the globe. We are all at risk when we purchase produce that is raised and sprayed with petrochemical products. Our commitment to active non-violent protest is to discontinue our purchasing of pesticide laden commercial agribusiness produce and demand that the federal government, and all our state governments, make it a priority to *protect* us and our environment from further harm. This is our right. If we do this we will be supporting farm workers around the world. It's the least we can do. As César Chavez stated, "All things are possible."

Food Declaration

Reprinted with permission from *www.fooddeclaration.org* Web site:
We, the undersigned, believe that a healthy food system is necessary to meet the urgent challenges of our time. Behind us stands more than a half-century of industrial food production, underwritten by cheap fossil fuels, abundant land and water resources, and a drive to maximize the global harvest of cheap resources, coupled with drive to maximize the global harvest of cheap calories. Ahead lie rising energy and food costs, a changing climate, declining water supplies, a growing population, and the paradox of widespread hunger and obesity.

These realities call for a radically different approach to food and agriculture. We believe the food system must be reorganized on a foundation of health: for our communities, for people, for animals, and for the natural world. The quality of food and not just the quantity ought to guide our agriculture. The ways we grow, distribute, and prepare food should celebrate our various cultures and our shared humanity, providing not only sustenance, but justice, beauty and pleasure.

Governments have a duty to protect people from malnutrition, unsafe food, and exploitation, and to protect the land and water, on which we depend, from degradation. Individuals, producers and organizations have a duty to create regional systems that can provide healthy food for their communities. We all have a duty to respect and honor the laborers of the land, without whom we could not survive. The changes we call for here have begun, but the time has come to accelerate the transformation of our food and agriculture and make its benefits available to all.

We believe that the following twelve principles should frame food and agriculture policy, to ensure that it will contribute to the health and wealth of the nation and the world.

A healthy food and agriculture policy:

1. Forms the foundation of secure and prosperous societies, healthy communities, and healthy people.

2. Provides access to affordable, nutritious food to everyone.

3. Prevents the exploitation of farmers, workers and natural resources; the domination of genomes and markets; and the cruel treatment of animals, by any nation, corporation or individual.

4. Upholds the dignity, safety, and quality of life for all who work to feed us.

5. Commits resources to teach children the skills and knowledge essential to food production, preparation, nutrition, and enjoyment.

6. Protects the finite resources of productive soils, fresh water, and biological diversity.

7. Strives to remove fossil fuel from every link in the food chain and replace it with renewable resources and energy.

8. Originates from a biological rather than an industrial framework.

9. Fosters diversity in all its relevant forms: diversity of domestic and wild species; diversity of foods, flavors and traditions; diversity of ownership.

10. Requires a national dialogue concerning technologies used in production, and allows regions to adopt their own respective guidelines on such matters.

11. Enforces transparency so that citizens know how their food is produced, where it comes from, and what it contains.

12. Promotes economic structures and supports programs to

nurture the development of just and sustainable regional farm and food networks.

Our pursuit of healthy food and agriculture unites us as people and as communities, across geographic boundaries, and social and economic lines. We pledge our votes, our purchases, our creativity and our energies to this urgent cause.

Sign the petition at *www.fooddeclaration.org*.

Introduction
Good Nutrition is a Way of Life

There were three books that influenced the way this cookbook came about and why the recipes contain specific ingredients while leaving others out. The first book was *The Schwarzbein Principle,* written by Dr. Diana Schwarzbein, a respected authority on the treatment of diabetes, addictions, weight loss, and the prevention and reversal of the degenerative diseases of aging. The second book, *The UltraMind Solution,* was written by Dr. Mark Hyman. Dr. Hyman reveals that the epidemic of brain problems (broken brains) we are facing as a society today, which include ADD/HD, autism and Aspberger's syndrome, bi-polar disorder, anxiety, insomnia, mood swings, Alzheimer's, Parkinson's and schizophrenia, are not the result of problems originating *inside* our brains and we are not suffering from a Prozac deficiency. These conditions result from foods and environmental sources, which we are ingesting that are toxic. The toxins then cross the blood brain barrier, which is more permeable than originally thought. After reading Dr. Hyman's book I began to suspect that my mother's life long illness with schizophrenia, which was diagnosed after we moved from Minnesota to California in 1952, was the result of a poor diet lacking in essential nutrients, coupled with smoking. Mother began smoking as a teenager.

I recall that the 1950s were the time when "food inventions" became popular and were being consumed by an unaware American public as safe (approved by the FDA). My early diet, and the diet of my three younger brothers, consisted of these *manufactured food products:* Velveeta Cheese, Crisco, margarine, Rainbow Bread, Skippy Peanut Butter (hydrogenated oil), bottled salad dressings with preservatives, and breakfast cereals containing mostly refined sugars and grains. We ate meat and poultry raised on grains grown with chemical fertilizers and pesticides. These "new" foods were a far cry from the real foods my mother was raised on in the small town of Sartell, Minnesota. Her father, Charles Sartell, had one of the biggest gardens in town during the Depression and he gave the extra vegetables to his neighbors. Mother's family had rich sources of real dairy products and they ate barnyard chicken and eggs. During the Depression, when meat sources were scarce, they ate meat (some squirrel I hear) procured from hunting. For fish they just walked across the street to the Mississippi River where my grandfather owned a lumber mill. Even though my grandfather lost his lumber mill in the Depression, their diet remained high in essential nutrients, comparatively speaking.

It was not until we moved to California and began eating the "new food inventions" that my mother's illness started. A genetic disorder, which runs in our family, known as *pyroluria* (where the body excretes essential zinc and vitamin B-6 through the urine) also contributed to the onset of the schizophrenia. People with schizophrenia should be tested for this condition as it requires lifelong supplementation with vitamin B-6 and zinc. It is also necessary to be tested for mercury as high concentrations of mercury in the body do not allow for the absorption of zinc. Due to the continued burning of coal as a source of planetary energy, we are now exposed to high levels of mercury in the atmosphere. All the industrial toxins released into the biosphere affect us in many ways.

Also, it is now scientifically proven that brain allergies and the lack of certain nutrients will contribute to the onset of many mental illnesses such as bi-polar disorder, autism, ADD/HD, depression, phobias, eating disorders, addictions, Alzheimer's, and anxiety. The list goes on and on. We now have evidence from scientific research and statistics (not to mention our national health costs) that most of our population has been suffering from a variety of physical and mental problems due to poor nutrition. Schizophrenia, being rare, is only one of them. It has been a lifelong quest of mine to know what caused my mother's schizophrenia. Now I feel that I have the answer. The answer is a genetic condition which *causes* vitamin B-6 and zinc deficiencies, smoking, and possible environmental toxins. Now we know from scientific research that most of the causes of mental disorders originate outside the brain and not within the brain itself.

Knowing that we have many toxins in our current food supply, I decided to write a cookbook based on what I understand the problem foods and food additives to be and advocate for the elimination of these substances from our cooking. I am primarily a chef with a thirty year background in cooking beginning with my first restaurant, Pauli's Café, founded in San Francisco in 1975. In 1980 I moved to the Napa Valley and ran a successful catering business, The Best of Everything, until I retired in 2003. My main expertise in writing this book comes from a very strong culinary background and not a scientific or medical background. I have always loved cooking.

I was right in the middle of writing this book when a Portland friend of mine handed me yet another book to read and said it would change my approach to what I was writing. I was not pleased, as things were going pretty well, or so I thought. This darned book was *Primal Body—Primal Mind*, by Nora Gedgaudas, a Portland-based neurofeedback specialist and board certified nutritional therapist. Nora has studied extensively the Paleolithic diet of our distant ancestors and her book explained quite clearly how our long biological history conditioned us to eat. *Primal Body—Primal Mind* stopped me dead in my tracks as I realized *grass-fed* meats (and their fats), wild-caught fish, nuts, seeds, and berries are the foods that our bodies and brains have flourished on for 100,000 generations of our evolution.

All three of the authors who influenced this cookbook, Dr. Schwarzbein, Dr. Hyman, and Nora Gedgaudas advocate eating a diet free from chemical food additives, refined grain products, sugars and trans-fats, in other words pre-packaged food products. Dr. Hyman and Ms. Gedgaudas are also strong proponents of eating animals and dairy products that are exclusively grass-fed or pastured. The meat and fats and dairy products of animals that are grass-fed are of utmost importance to our diet because they retain essential nutrients, most importantly the Omega-3 fatty acids and L-Tryptophan, an essential amino acid that makes serotonin in the body. Our current American diet is sorely lacking in these essential nutrients and we have to pay attention now to make sure we choose to include meat, fish, and dairy that contain these nutrients in our diet.

I would say the major difference in what the authors have advocated is that Nora strongly recommends not eating grains at all. There is scientific evidence to support the fact that our ancestors did not eat plants because they did not cook. Only cooking would have removed toxins from the plants and since our ancestors didn't cook, plants were avoided. We know that farming grains began about 10,000 years ago and has been prevalent in Europe for only 2000 years. Because of this we do not genetically require grains in our diet. Our human brain did not evolve from grain consumption. It evolved from eating wild meat and fish and a significant amount of their accompanying fats. As I was reading all this it made a lot of sense. Our ancestors did not eat carbohydrates; they ate protein and fat. As a result of reading *Primal Body— Primal Mind* I have modified the recipes in this book to reduce grain consumption.

When I found out recently I was hypoglycemic I also decided to reduce carbohydrates in my diet. Just eliminating the obvious refined sugar, honey, and maple syrup was not enough. I also had to eliminate those foods that easily convert to sugar when consumed, like bread, rice, potatoes, and pasta. Doing this has made a huge difference in my health and level of energy. People who are diabetic or have allergies to grains know what I'm talking about, but anyone can try this and see how it feels for them.

Good nutrition is a *way* of life. Once you are on this way and begin to experience the lasting health benefits of eating nutrient dense protein, healthy fats, and organic whole foods, you will never go back to your former eating habits again. Having optimum nutrition to fuel your life is actually easier than you think. The best way to begin is to make the decision that this is essential and no longer an option and you are truly committed to your well being, then begin to take the steps based on that decision. If you are reading this book at all, chances are you have an interest in your health. The purpose of this book is to help you make the change to a new way of eating, simply and deliciously. This is going to be an interesting, fun, and rewarding adventure.

Learning to eat sustainably is a *beginning* step. With anything new, the first thing to do is to be interested and then become more informed. In the following pages I have provided lots of information, some of which you may already be familiar. Please keep your mind open and test everything by how you are feeling once you are eating according to the sustainable plan. By cooking the recipes in the book you will still be eating your favorite foods, but with the harmful ingredients (like gluten, refined flour and sugar, bad oils and trans-fats, high fructose corn syrup, and preservatives) eliminated. When you make the recipes they will only taste *better* than before. If you have friends over for dinner they won't notice you have removed harmful ingredients and substituted healthy ones. But they just might be aware they are eating food that is vibrant, delicious, and healthy.

In feeding our bodies, according to the sustainable plan, I am proposing that we are also taking care of our earth as well. For instance, by eliminating grain-fed meat from our diet we are conserving precious water. It takes huge amounts of water to grow the grains that feed large animals. The genetically modified grain is raised with petrochemicals and fertilizers that ruin our soil and create disaster in the environment. Most of the animals we consume are raised in unsanitary conditions on huge feedlots. During this finishing time (when they are fed grains) they are prone to illness so they are given hormones and antibiotics. These animals live a life under deplorable conditions, which we can no longer in good conscience support. Our rivers and oceans are now filled with these runoff antibiotics and chemicals. Every food choice we make now will either contribute to the overall environmental problems we are facing as a species or help to eradicate it. We must choose and time is of the essence. We can no longer afford to be oblivious to the maintenance of a healthy planet.

I ask you to purchase only meats that are entirely *grass-fed* (no grain finishing at all) and insist that your grocery story carry these meats. Please choose *pastured* chickens and turkeys when you can find them and, once again, please let your grocer know that you want to have these items in the store. Purchase only line-caught wild fish that are not on the endangered species list as your contribution to saving the oceans for future generations. We now know that smaller amounts of nutrient dense protein such as 2 or 3 ounces per meal are better for us than the larger portions we have been used to eating. In fact eating too much meat is actually counterproductive to health. Eating less of these precious and *expensive* protein sources is also going to be a huge savings. Please use the resources at the end of the book to locate grass-fed meats in your area.

One of the main reasons to buy organic foods is that the toxic petrochemicals, used to grow crops, cause illnesses for many farm workers and their children world wide every year. These biohazards also ruin our soil. It takes years to rebuild soil that has been damaged by petro-fertilizers. If you ever fly over California you will see huge areas where the soil has become an ugly dead wasteland due to the use of these products. The effect these poisons have on migrating birds and wildlife has eradicated thousands of species from the earth and they just may be eradicating us as well, but more slowly. The Sacramento River Delta, which is the western hemisphere's largest river delta, and the stopping place of many bird species is now in severe decline due to pollutants and the diversion of water from the Sacramento River to Southern California. To lose the delta will be a major environmental catastrophe.

It may seem like a big sacrifice to make significant dietary changes but the benefits are going to go beyond what you can imagine for the *whole earth*. We must begin to take into account the global impact of all of our purchases, especially food, which we have to buy every day. In addition to being healthier, there are other benefits to you, not the least of which is the *expense of eating large quantities of meat*. In this book I have reduced the amounts of the meat, poultry, or fish originally called for in the recipes but you will not be suffering from lack of protein in your diet. By eating according to the sustainable diet plan you will be maximizing your nutrient intake and at the same time find your food dollar is going to stretch further.

Pauli Halstead
Hood River, Oregon

Setting the Stage for Success

Make the kitchen your favorite room in the house so it will be a pleasure to be there. Have relaxing music playing while you cook. Organize your cooking tools attractively in containers that are handy to the stove. Have your good oils, Celtic sea salt, and pepper grinder at hand as well. You are an artist. Your ingredients are your artist's palette.

Getting your kitchen ready with the right tools
The right cooking tools will contribute to your overall success and add to your cooking enjoyment. Quality tools will last a lifetime if you take proper care of them.

These are my recommendations:
- small kitchen ounce scale, optional
- instant read meat thermometer
- candy thermometer (for making yogurt)
- good quality knives (you don't need many). Two sizes of chef's knives, a meat slicer & a paring knife
- small plastic cutting boards that can go in the dishwasher. Various colors for meats & veggies
- large stainless steel stock pot with lid
- 2 & 4 quart stainless steel saucepans with lids
- 8 & 12 inch sauté pans, heavy bottomed stainless steel, or titanium non-stick cookware (Stainless cookware reasonably priced from *www.Overstock.com*. Titanium cookware at "just pots" *www.justpotsonline.*)
- food processor
- blender
- coffee grinder for spices and sesame/flaxseed mix
- several sizes wire whisks
- non-meltable rubber spatulas

- ▶ assorted measuring cups and measuring spoons
- ▶ microplaners/graters for grating ginger and lemon zest
- ▶ two heavy stainless steel sheet pans
- ▶ two 9 x 13 inch rectangular glass baking dishes
- ▶ two 9 or 10 inch glass pie pans
- ▶ several sizes of fluted tart pans (optional)
- ▶ nut milk bag (optional)
- ▶ Spiralizer, "turning slicer" available at *www.sunfood.com, www. discountjuicers.com, www.rawgourmet.com*

Throwing away the trash:

The first thing to do before you go shopping for the wonderful new *sustainable plan* foods is get rid of the things you will not be using any longer. You will be throwing away processed, packaged, junk (most snack items), and fast foods. Don't be afraid to be ruthless. *Reading labels is the key.* By eliminating the foods that are not on your plan you will be making space in your refrigerator and your pantry for the sustainable, healthy foods.

We have become a nation who has managed to become both overfed and undernourished. Our brains have become addicted to foods that are refined and are easily reduced to pure glucose.

Learning to shop for health:

Fortunately we now have stores like Whole Foods, Trader Joe's, New Seasons, and Wild Oats, which carry most of the products that will make it easy for you to do your shopping. Even major stores, like Safeway and Costco are joining the organic mainstream. Be active and tell your grocery store manager what you want. Many cities now have farmer's markets, which are a lot of fun and also educational. The main focus, other than reading labels, is to buy organic foods as much as possible. It is also important that dairy, eggs, and poultry are antibiotic and hormone free and the meats you buy are *entirely grass fed*. If you eat fish avoid farm raised and buy only line-caught wild fish.

Food Processing and its impact on the environment:

Every year we contribute mountains of metal, glass, paper, cardboard, and plastic to our growing landfills. Even if we recycle this practice of packaging everything costs us in ways that we don't realize. It's just not an out of sight, out of mind problem. The cost of transporting all this packaged food (and then the resulting garbage and recycling) in terms of the use of oil cannot be overlooked. This is a major reason to stop using pre-packaged foods as much as possible. Buy fresh whole foods and buy in bulk whenever possible. Grow your own herbs and vegetables. Buy at the farmer's market or a local producer near you to cut down on transportation costs. Read *Animal, Vegetable, Miracle* by Barbara Kingsolver and try her example. Make a decision on what you can live without. Take a look at each product you use and try to choose items that come from the state in which you live.

Red flags in labeling:

The consequences of not knowing what food additives can do to your health nowadays are too risky. *We must be informed.* The Food and Drug Administration (FDA) still allows many harmful and potentially deadly substances to be added to our national food supply. This has to stop and the public must demand changes. For the time being the only thing we can do is to not purchase products with dangerous additives. *Think about what these additives are doing to our growing children and how they might be affecting their developing brains.*

The dangerous substances to avoid are:

- high fructose corn syrup (toxic and deadly)
- high sugar content (sugars) *refined **and** naturally occurring sugars (honey, maple syrup, agave)*
- hydrogenated or partially hydrogenated oils (avoid artificial trans-fats and rancid fats)
- high carbohydrate content (avoid "processed" carbohydrates). No white stuff!
- food colorings and artificial flavorings

- high salt (sodium)
- chemical preservatives, MSG, nitrates, benzoic acid, sulfur dioxide
- *gluten* (if you are gluten sensitive)
- foods you may be allergic to such as dairy, soy, nuts, or eggs. You may need to be tested for food allergies, which contribute to many serious physical and mental illnesses (yes, brain problems)
- avoid foods with low or no fiber (a high fiber diet is essential for good health)
- grains and legumes which have not been presoaked
- genetically modified grains

Our ancestors consumed less than 20 teaspoons of sugar a year. The average American now consumes almost a half-pound of sugar per day. No wonder we have the sugar blues.

Preservatives in Food
If it doesn't look like food, it probably isn't

Preservatives are additives in food, which help to stop food from spoiling. Unfortunately many of these substances are highly toxic and can cause allergic reactions, illness, and even death. The Food Allergen Labeling and Consumer Protection Act of 2004 *requires* food manufacturers to disclose the eight most common allergens on the labels of packaged foods. The only problem with this is it's not very well monitored and also the manufacturers do not have to disclose an ingredient until a certain percentage is present in the food. So, we need to be *very* vigilant, especially when it comes to protecting our children and their developing brains.

Nitrates are used to preserve meats and are found in lunchmeats, ham and bacon products. Nitrates can cause asthma, nausea, vomiting, and headaches.

Sulfites (which are found in wines) can also cause some of the same symptoms as nitrates. Sulfites are used to prevent fungal spoilage, as well as the browning, which occurs on fruits and vegetables.

Sodium Nitrite is capable of being converted to nitrous acid when ingested. Animal testing has shown that nitrous acid caused high rates of cancer in animals but it is still in use.

Benzoic acid, also known as sodium benzoate, is added to margarine, fruit juices, and carbonated beverages. It has been known to cause severe allergic reaction and death.

Sulfur Dioxide is a toxin used to preserve dried fruits and molasses. It is used to prevent brown spots on fresh fruits and vegetables such as apple and potatoes. Sulfur dioxide bleaches out rot, hiding inferior fruits and vegetables and destroying the vitamin B's in produce.

Artificial Sweeteners: Saccharine and aspartame have been linked to behavioral problems, hyperactivity, and allergies. Saccharin was shown to increase bladder cancer in animal testing and is, therefore, required to carry a warning label.

Monosodium Glutamate had been banned in baby food but now it's back. It's being sprayed on fruits, nuts, vegetables and grains, which are then *used in baby food,* and it's still in wide use in other food products as well. Processed *free glutamic acid* is the reactive component in "monosodium glutamate." Synthetic MSG, free glutamic acid, is now being sprayed on all kinds of crops. Called AuxiGro WP Plant Metabolic Primer, it's manufactured by Emerald Bio Agriculture. Children are eating the fruits and vegetables sprayed with this product. Free glutamic acid is known to be toxic to the nervous system. As yet no one knows what the long terms affects of this substance are which is one more reason to buy organic only.

Artificial Flavors have been linked to allergic reactions and behavioral problems. There are over 200 of them in use. These flavorings are not required to be listed in detail because the Food and Drug Administration recognizes them as safe.

Emulsifiers, Stabilizers, and Thickeners: Propylene glycol is a synthetic solvent used as an emulsifier in food and is recognized as toxic to the skin. It is also considered to be a neurological toxicant. The Food and Drug Administration still recognizes it as safe. Many vitamins contain this ingredient so watch out for it.

Refined Foods: Refined flours, which are found in white breads, white rice, pasta, cookies, and numerous junk foods are wreaking havoc in the world. With the brown husk of the grain removed, the remaining refined starches are broken down quickly into sugar and absorbed immediately into the blood stream causing glucose levels to rise, thus increasing the risk of obesity. Refining destroys most of the nutrients in the foods. Healthy unsaturated fatty acids are lost during the milling process. Vitamin E is significantly destroyed. Other nutrients such as vitamins and minerals are also lost.

Bleaching is used to process wheat into commercial baked goods. Various chemical bleaching agents such as **oxide of nitrogen**, **chlorine**, **chloride, nitrosyl**, and **benzoyl peroxide** are mixed with a wide variety of chemical salts. Chloride oxide, which catalyzes a chemical reaction that destroys beta cells in the pancreas is now being linked to diabetes. Even though the toxicity of chloride oxide is recognized, the FDA still allows its use.

Gluten: According to Dr. Mark Hyman, *The UltraMind Solution*, **"Gluten is one common factor that can create so many illnesses it would be hard to count them all."** For those who are gluten sensitive you can go to The Celiac Spru Association Web site, or (*www.celiac.com*) for lists of gluten containing foods. Some of these are wheat, barley, oats, spelt, triticale, kamut, and rye.

A gluten-free diet will require a completely new approach to eating that will affect a person's entire life. People with celiac disease have to be extremely careful about what they buy for lunch at school or work, eat at cocktail parties, or grab from the refrigerator for a midnight snack. Dining out can be challenging as the person with celiac disease must learn how to scrutinize the menu for foods with gluten and question the waiter about possible hidden sources of gluten. With practice, identifying potential sources of gluten will become second nature and people will learn how to recognize which foods are safe and which are off limits.

Commercial Dairy Products may contain gluten as an additive. Do not buy dairy products such as cheese spreads, chip & dip products, and ice creams that have vegetable gum or modified food starch and preservatives. Do not use non-dairy creamers. Read labels carefully.

Bottled Salad Dressings are to be eliminated. They may have a label that says, "all natural" but these are the ingredients on a label I have right here on my desk. "Water, soybean oil, buttermilk, maltodextrin, sugar, salt, less than 2% dried spices, dried garlic, natural flavors, (soy) egg yolk, modified food starch, soy lecithin, celery puree, corn oil, carrageenan, carrot puree, dried onion, onion puree, phosphoric acid, vinegar, artificial flavor, disodium phosphate, xanthan gum, monosodium glutamate, artificial color, disodium inosinate, disodium guanylate with sorbic acid, potassium sorbate, and calcium disodium EDTA added as a preservatives." **Yuk!** Why would you want to eat that horrible stuff? Make your own homemade dressing and your salads will taste fabulous.

Beverages to Avoid would be all carbonated beverages, instant drinks, and drinks that are processed with additives, emulsifiers, and stabilizers. Do not buy instant coffees or teas, cocoa mixes with sugar and artificial flavorings, flavored malted milk, commercial chocolate milk, and ground coffees, which contain grains and artificial flavors. *Do not buy your children harmful beverages with high fructose corn syrup and artificial flavors and colors. All those ingredients are toxins that go through the blood/brain barrier and affect brain functioning.*

All Commercially Made Pies, Cakes, and Pastries should be completely eliminated from your diet. It's safe to say that the rise of diabetes in this country, as well as many other diseases are caused by the consumption of these products. It's very difficult to break the habit of eating these foods (if you can even call them foods) because we are so much in the habit of continually treating ourselves to sugar and carbohydrates when we're under stress. But, these foods actually increase stress. *Of all the addictions, including addiction to alcohol and other drugs, sugar is one of the toughest to quit.* I know from experience. It has taken me most of a lifetime to break this habit and I sympathize with everyone who has to face it. But *now* is the time to do it. You can do it if you *clean house* and only have "safe" foods at home. This goes for your children as well. You do not want to raise children who are addicted to sugar and refined carbohydrates. It's now known that autism, ADD, and ADHD are caused by sugar, refined carbohydrates, gluten, and food allergies. Please read *The UltraMind Solution* by Dr. Mark Hyman.

All Processed Luncheon Meats, Smoked Meats, and Sausages should also be cast out of your refrigerator. Many of these products contain sodium nitrates, grain fillers, artificial colorings, and flavors. Your Thanksgiving turkey, if it is injected with a basting liquid, is probably toxic. Only buy *pastured*, organic or preferably wild turkeys. There are organic sausages with no grain fillers, such as Bruce Aidell's Organic Chicken Sausages. Amylu Chicken Sausages are entirely *gluten free* and pork casing free. *www.SausagesbyAmylu.com*

Grain Fed Animals: Excerpted with permission from Jo Robinson's Web site, *www.eatwild.com.*

Feedlot diets are a recipe for animal discomfort and disease. As consumers we have to realize that taking ruminants off their natural diet of pasture and fattening them on grain or other feed diminishes the nutritional value of the meat and milk. But what does a feedlot diet do to the health and well-being of the animals?

1) The first negative consequence of a feedlot diet is a condition called "acidosis." During the normal digestive process, bacteria in the rumen of cattle, bison, or sheep produce a variety of acids. When animals are kept on pasture, they produce copious amounts of saliva that neutralize the acidity. A feedlot diet is low in roughage, so the animals do not ruminate as long nor produce as much saliva. The net result is "acid indigestion."

2) Over time, acidosis can lead to a condition called "rumenitis," which is an inflammation of the wall of the rumen. The inflammation is caused by too much acid and too little roughage. Eventually, the wall of the rumen becomes ulcerated and no longer absorbs nutrients as efficiently.

3) Liver abscesses are a direct consequence of rumenitis. As the rumen wall becomes ulcerated, bacteria are able to pass through the walls and enter the bloodstream. Ultimately, the bacteria are transported to the liver where they

cause abscesses. From 15 to 30% of feedlot cattle have liver abscesses.

4) Bloat is a fourth consequence of a feedlot diet. All ruminants produce gas as a by-product of digestion. When they are on pasture, they belch up the gas without any difficulty. When they are switched to an artificial diet of grain the gasses can become trapped by a dense mat of foam. In serious cases of bloat, the rumen becomes so distended with gas that the animal is unable to breathe and dies from asphyxiation.

5) Feedlot polio is yet another direct consequence of switching animals from pasture to grain. When the rumen becomes too acidic, an enzyme called "thiaminase" is produced which destroys thiamin or vitamin B-1. The lack of vitamin B-1 starves the brain of energy and creates paralysis. Cattle that are suffering from feedlot polio are referred to as "brainers." Typically, feedlot managers try to manage these grain-caused problems with a medicine chest of drugs, including ionophores (to buffer acidity) and antibiotics (to reduce liver abscesses). A more sensible and humane approach is to feed animals their natural diet of pasture, to which they are superbly adapted.

Eating excess carbohydrates every day has a cumulative effect on the human body. "Choose carefully" which carbohydrates you will eat during the day. Please remember all the systems in the body are connected. Proper nutrition can balance your metabolism, improve your mood, and perhaps save your life.

Other Facts to Consider

Children Do Not Have to Be Overweight

In chapter twenty of her book, *The Schwarzbein Principle*, Dr. Diana Schwarzbein reminds us that we have moved further away from the diets of our ancestors by feeding our children processed junk foods. It is common practice by food manufacturers to remove the fats from these food products. These products contain harmful chemicals or more sugar to add flavor. According to Dr. Schwarzbein, "These processed foods are fattening, first, because they contain more sugar, which raises insulin levels and, second, because they instigate the vicious cycle of carbohydrate craving. This is why many children are overweight today. **To make matters worse, children now eat low-fat foods**. Unfortunately, we have been taught to worry more about the fat content than the chemical and sugar content of these foods. We have been led to believe that, as long as there is little or no fat, we are doing no harm.

Dr. Schwarzbein also states that "Adults need fat in their diet to replenish and nourish the body, but children need fat even more to develop into healthy adults. Fatty foods are the source of the fat-soluble vitamins A, E, D, and K. Taking vitamin supplements has not shown the same health benefits as eating the fatty foods that contain these fat-soluble vitamins. "When children come to me for 'genetic obesity,' I immediately switch them to a balanced diet sufficient in proteins and fats while decreasing their carbohydrate consumption. Every one of these children loses body fat and gains her or his ideal body composition." *www.schwarzbeinprinciple.com*

The closer you can come to eliminating all forms of sugar and starch (including grains, bread, pasta, rice, potatoes, desserts, juices, alcohol, honey, maple syrup . . . etc.) by far the better.
—Nora Gedgaudas, *Primal Body—Primal Mind*

Hypoglycemia: Recognizing many of the symptoms of hypoglycemia in myself and my family I decided to change my eating habits and also supplement my diet with essential vitamins and minerals.

What are the symptoms of hypoglycemia?
According to Nora Gedgaudas:

> When cells utilize available glucose so rapidly that the blood cannot readily meet the constant demand for more fuel, the cells actually become starved. Glucose deficiency drastically alters the function of the brain, since the brain cells cannot store glucose and thus require a continuous supply to generate energy. In a state of glucose starvation, the brain suffers reduced efficiency and can no longer direct vital processes, thus disrupting physical and emotional behavior.

Physical and emotional disturbances in the hypoglycemic disorders vary according to the severity of the disorder and the individual affected. Mental symptoms frequently resulting from hypoglycemia include:

anxiety	headaches
fatigue	irritability
nervousness	depression
crying spells	mental confusion or forgetfulness
insomnia	phobias and fears
disruptive outbursts	dis-perceptions
dizziness, vertigo, faintness	
low blood pressure, cold hands and feet	

Hypoglycemia is easy to treat:
▶ small amounts, 2–3 ounces of nutrient dense protein (eggs, tuna, fish, chicken, meat) at each meal.

- only very small amounts of complex carbohydrates (sprouted grain bread, non-gluten whole grains) which have been soaked for at least 8 hours before cooking).
- higher quality fat intake (in small amounts and in the *absence of refined sugars and flour)*. Butter from grass-fed cows, organic olive oil, coconut oil, and cold pressed sesame oil. (No canola, soy, peanut oil, safflower oil, hemp or corn oils, including store bought mayonnaise, margarine, and salad dressings**)**.
- increase vitamin and mineral supplementation.
- lots of non-starchy veggies.
- at least one "green drink" (super-food) per day for increased vitamins and minerals.
- *eliminate junk foods, wine (high in sugar), all "white stuff," candy, cookies.*
- snacks can be a small piece of raw cheese, New Zealand grass-fed cheddar or goat cheese, a hard boiled egg, a spoonful of almond butter, a few almonds. **NO** raisins, dried cranberries or any dried fruit, which are extremely high in sugar (28 grams per serving), and should not be eaten if hypoglycemic.

Type 2 Diabetes

The Center for Disease Control estimates that if current dietary habits persist as many as one third of this nation's kids will become diabetic. The major cause is a form of malnutrition tied to highly processed, pre-packaged and fast foods that are high in refined sugar and trans-fats and short on vitamins and complex carbohydrates. The national costs of caring for tens of millions of Type 2 diabetics is draining public coffers and personal wealth.

According to Dr. Gabriel Cousens, from the Tree of Life Web site, "Worldwide diabetes has reached pandemic proportions. According to the American Diabetes Association, diabetes now affects close to 20 million people in the United States and that figure remains on the rise, and 20 million pre-diabetics in America, the same in Europe and more in India and China. At the current trend 1 in 3 children born after 2000 will have diabetes, but it was under 1 in 100 at the turn of the century. Yet still many say life-long medication is required and diabetes is 'incurable' by nutrition." Dr. Cousens proposes that diabetes can be cured in a relatively short time with a raw food diet.

Dr. Diana Schwarzbein also teaches that Type 2 diabetes can be greatly alleviated and even cured by proper diet. Please read *The Schwarzbein Principle*. Dr. Schwarzbein is the founder of the Endocrinology Institute of Santa Barbara. She sub-specializes in metabolism, diabetes, osteoporosis, menopause, and thyroid conditions.

Cereal Grains and Legumes: The following is from Nora Gedgaudas in *Primal Body—Primal Mind*.

Grains and legumes typically contain very high levels of a substance known as *phytic acid*. Phytic acid actively binds minerals and eliminates them from the body and results, *with increasing consumption*, in widespread mineral deficiencies, including calcium, iron, magnesium, and zinc. Legumes typically containing 60% starch and only relatively small amounts of *incomplete* protein also contain potent protease inhibitors, which can damage one's ability to digest and utilize dietary protein, as well as damage the pancreas over time.

Careful preparation by pre-soaking, sprouting, or fermenting these foods can minimize or even eliminate phytic acid and other anti-nutrients. Nonetheless, they remain a very high carbohydrate food source.

Grains and legumes also contain goitrogens, or thyroid-inhibiting substances, as well as "foreign proteins" like gluten, and are an extremely common source of allergies and sensitivities that can lead to both physical and mental or emotional disorders, even when the best preparation methods are used. One additional hypothesis suggests that the lack of L-tryptophan in grains, now an unnatural source for commercially raised beef and poultry (not to mention humans), may help account for the rampant serotonin deficiencies, clinical depression, anxiety, and some forms of ADD in our populations. Carbohydrate consumption, in general, depletes serotonin stores, as well as greatly depletes the B-vitamins needed to convert amino acids to many needed neurotransmitters.

As there is *no human dietary grain requirement*—and since grain consumption causes so many known health problems due to its anti-nutrient content, its tryptophan poor profile, high omega-6 levels and its mainly starch based content, as well as its allergy and sensitivity potential—there is little reason to include grains in the diet of anyone seeking optimal health.

In fact, the fewer grains consumed the better. Zero is by far the best.

Brain and mood disorders, osteoporosis, diabetes, cardiovascular diseases, bowel diseases, autoimmune diseases, inflammatory disorders, and cancer are rampant. Grains are rarely suspected as the original culprit, though every one of these disorders can potentially be traced to often-insidious gluten intolerance. **Gluten sensitivity is only rarely obvious to the afflicted,** and many are even surprised to learn they have this sensitivity.

Even though other grains such as quinoa, millet, and buckwheat do not contain gluten, they are still more a source of starch than of protein. Gluten and carbohydrate intolerance, in general, are far more the rule than the exception in today's world. It is logical to conclude that grain consumption, especially gluten-containing grains, just isn't worth the dietary risk, given our culture's innumerable health challenges and vulnerabilities. Why play Russian roulette? Why add to the unnecessary, glycating, fattening, and neurotransmitter and hormonally dysregulating carbohydrate load?

After reading Dr. Diana Schwarzbein's book, *The Schwarzbein Principle,* and Dr. Mark Hyman's book the *UltraMind Solution*, and *Primal*

Body—Primal Mind, I have become convinced that our **cumulative carbohydrate consumption** in the United States is the cause of many diseases, including rampant mental illnesses and depression. According to Dr. Hyman, our "brains are broken" because of our body's allergic reaction to gluten and other toxic substances which we are ingesting. I would also like to remind everyone again that *our children and their developing brains are especially vulnerable.* Children are much more intolerant of grains and legumes, starch, milk, and sugars (including honey, maple syrup, agave, most fruits, and juices).

The research is in, the scientific papers have been written and published and now the facts are known. We can no longer say we didn't have the correct information. Therefore, in this book, I have eliminated or greatly reduced grains, legumes, and sugars from the recipes. This book is meant to be a transition to a new sustainable way of eating, so I leave it up to you to read and then to test what these experts are saying by trying the *sustainable* eating plan. If you choose to eat some selected grains such as quinoa, brown rice, or wild rice, then follow the recommendations for soaking and eat the grains "in moderation." It's much healthier to get your carbohydrates from non-starchy vegetables, coconut milk, berries, seeds, and nuts than from grains.

Cholesterol: From the chapter, "Dispelling the Cholesterol Myth" in *Primal Body—Primal Mind*, here are a few quotes from Nora Gedgaudas.

Cholesterol is a vital substance in the human body. Using cholesterol, the body produces a series of stress-combating hormones and mediates the health and efficiency of the cell membranes.

Cholesterol is also essential for brain function and development. It forms membranes inside cells and keeps cell membranes permeable. It keeps moods level by stabilizing neurotransmitters and helps maintain a healthy immune system. No steroidal hormone can be manufactured without it, including estrogen, progesterone, testosterone, adresnaline, cortisol, and dehydroepeiandrosterone (DHEA).

Despite the body's ability to manufacture its own cholesterol it is very critical to supplement cholesterol in the diet. Historically the human diet has always contained significant amounts of cholesterol. Restricting or eliminating its intake indicates a crisis or famine to the body. The result is the production of a liver enzyme called *HMG-CoA reductase* that, in effect, then overproduces cholesterol from carbohydrates in the diet. Consuming carbohydrates in the diet while decreasing cholesterol intake guarantees a steady overproduction of cholesterol in the body. The only way to switch this overproduction off is to consume an adequate amount of dietary cholesterol and *back off the carbs.*

Soy Alert! The Weston A. Price Foundation is a non-profit nutrition education foundation dedicated to restoring nutrient dense foods to the human diet through education, research, and activism. The Foundation is spearheading a national campaign to warn consumers about the dangers of modern soy foods. Please visit their Web site *www.westonaprice. org* to learn more about the Foundation's Soy Alert campaign.

Soy has never been given Generally Recognized as Safe status (GRAS) by the FDA.

In the chapter on soy in *Primal Body—Primal Mind*, Nora Gedgaudas states,

Soy, (particularly tofu, soy milk, and soy protein isolate) is among the newest additions to the human diet. Soy has been considered unfit for human consumption since ancient times but chemical processing methods created by corporate interests have created an "all new" soy, purported to be the cornerstone of heath and longevity. The unsuspecting public has unfortunately succumbed to misleading claims and other marketing ploys to increasingly seek out meat substitutes—including texturized protein (TVP), tofu, soy milk, and soy protein powders. Many have been led to believe that these foods somehow prevent cancer and heart disease, and provide improved quality protein in their diets. *Nothing could be further from the truth.*

Soy contains the highest levels of phytic acid of any grain or legume. It is known that the high levels of phytic acid in soy will reduce the assimilation of minerals such as calcium, magnesium, copper, iron, and zinc and the phytic acid is *not* neutralized by soaking, or sprouting, or long term cooking either. Soy is a phyto-endocrine disrupter, inhibiting the thyroid enzyme, thyroid peroxidase, necessary for the synthesis of the hormones T3 and T4. Effects include autoimmune thyroiditis (Divi at al., 1997, 1996) and hypothyroidism involving obesity, dry skin, and hair, low blood pressure, slow pulse, depressed muscular activity, intolerance to cold, goiter, and sluggishness of physiological functions.

The only comparatively "safe" soy includes its fermented forms of miso, nato, and tempeh. Fermentation—and fermentation only—largely neutralizes trypsin inhibitors and phytic acid. Goitrogens or thyroid inhibitors, however, remain intact even following fermentation, so care must be given to not over-consume even these soy foods.

For the reasons mentioned above, and many other reasons stated in Ms. Gedgaudas' chapter on soy, you will not find soy as an ingredient in this book with the exception of Nama Shoyu soy sauce, San-J *wheat free* tamari and non-GMO organic miso.

Sodium: Processed foods tend to have more sodium. Too much sodium should be avoided since such an excess can cause damage to the heart and kidneys.

Water: I cannot overemphasize the importance of *pure water* in your diet and especially for the health of your growing children. Our current water supplies in the United States have been exposed to pesticides, pharmaceuticals (antibiotics are now in our water supply), heavy metals, harmful microbes, and other toxins. It is highly recommended to use a water filter (this could be an inexpensive Brita which uses a carbon filter) or a reverse osmosis filter, which can be installed in your home. I recommend that you do not buy water in plastic bottles as the plastic contains toxic phthalates or bisphenol. Use your filtered water to cook with and to make coffee, iced teas, and other beverages that you and your family consume. Always have the filtered water sitting out where the children can help themselves. See the resources section for Brita and reverse osmosis water filters. You may want to get your water tested. Please go to the Basic Laboratory (full-service environmental testing) Web site and order a test kit. *www.basiclab.com*

Microwave ovens: It is best not to use microwave ovens for much of your cooking. Microwaved food may increase instances of oxidative stress and inflammation in the body tissues. Only use the microwave to heat leftovers or to heat beverages.

Charcoal Grilled Food: There is evidence that charbroiled foods may increase the risk of cancer, so it is probably best to keep charcoal grilled foods to a minimum.

Mercury: A new study in the Pacific Ocean suggests that algae at the water's surface absorb mercury from the atmosphere and then sinks to mid-depths, where they decompose and release methylmercury, a highly toxic form of the metal that poisons both fish and the people who eat them. Mercury concentrations have increased in the Pacific by 30% in the last 20 years, the study found and if emissions continue to rise as expected, the scientists predict another 50% jump by 2050.

"We can now explain why large predatory fish in the open oceans have methylmercury in the first place," said Dave Krabbenhoft, a geo-chemist with the United States Geological Survey in Middleton, Wisc. "We don't have to scratch our heads anymore."

"Mercury is a byproduct of coal combustion, industrial waste, and other human activities. It is also a powerful neurotoxin that can cause developmental problems in babies and heart disease in adults, among other health woes. More than 90% of methylmercury that gets into people in the United States comes from ocean fish and shellfish, especially tuna."—by Emily Sohn. Visit original article at Discovery Channel.

From the Blue Ocean Web site on mercury: "Consumers get as much as 87% of their mercury intake from eating seafood. An EPA scientist estimated that one in six pregnant women has enough mercury in her blood to pose neurological threats to her developing baby. Mercury in adults causes impaired coordination, tremors, irritability, memory loss, depression, and blurred vision. Mercury's effects are even faster and worse in children." *www.safeseafoodapp.com* Please go to the Blue Ocean Institute's Web site and view the Blue Ocean Mercury Video. *www.blueocean.org/seafood*

Genetic Engineering of Plants and Animals: Genetic engineering may be one of our most challenging environmental problems in this century. This technology has already invaded our food supply, altering some of our most important staple food crops. Scientists have been able to take genetic material from one organism and insert it into the permanent genetic code of another. The resulting alarming creations are now being patented and released into the environment.

Up to 40 percent of U.S. corn and 80% of soybeans are genetically engineered. The current estimate is that 60% of the processed foods on our grocery store shelves contain these genetically engineered ingredients.

A number of recent studies have shown that genetically engineered foods can result in serious health risks to humans, not to mention domestic and wild animals. Health risks can include increased allergies, antibiotic resistance, immune system suppression, and even cancer. *It has now been reported that the use of genetically engineered crops could lead to uncontrolled biological pollution and the contamination of non-genetically engineered life forms.*

The Center for Food Safety is seeking to halt the approval, commercialization or release of any new genetically engineered crops until they have been proven safe or human consumption and the environment. All of us must demand that our Congress pass laws that food products, which contain genetically engineered ingredients, be clearly labeled. We must also seek to limit and reduce the proliferation of genetically engineered crops. Visit *www.centerforfoodsafety.org/geneticall2.cfm*

Propylene Oxide Gas (PPO) is sometimes used to sterilize nuts from bacteria. Be sure not to buy any nuts that have been treated with this chemical. It is a known carcinogen. It is toxic and poisonous. The European Union has prohibited the use of PPO Gas on any Human Food Product. The USDA and FDA still allow it. Inquire at your store if their fruits and nuts have been exposed to PPO.

Antibiotics in Our Food Supply: Many consumers are concerned about the health implications of antibiotic overuse. Their overuse in farm animals may mean the next time you need to take antibiotics, they just might not work.

The Campaign to End Antibiotic Overuse—We have a right to know. We all need to urge USDA to rethink and clarify labels and claims relevant to antibiotic resistance. We must be diligent in protecting the public health at all times. KAW is a coalition of health, environmental, consumer, human, religious, and other advocacy groups that have over nine million members. *www.keepanitbioticsworking.com*

From the KAW Web site:

KAW believes that meat labels giving consumers choices of products produced with reduced antibiotics could help accomplish the public health goal of reducing the use of antibiotics in animal agriculture. To work to that end, however, claims and standards must be clear and relevant to consumer interests. In addition, the claims must serve to distinguish "alternative" animal production practices from "conventional" practices that involve heavy or routine use of antibiotics. Label claims that obscure important differences between conventional and alternative production systems will deny customers the freedom they want and label clarity they have a right to expect—the freedom to discern and choose between the products from these different kinds of systems. In addition, unclear label claims undercut the ability of alternative producers to fairly compete for customers by making it harder for these producers to differentiate their products. By so doing, such claims put at risk the livelihoods of farmers who have staked their financial futures on raising animals without the use of antibiotics.

Synthetic Hormone Usage in Dairy Cows: According to the Organic Consumers Association there are many reasons to avoid consuming dairy products with the synthetic hormone rBGH.

- rBGH makes cows sick. Monsanto (the makers of the synthetic hormone POSILAC) has been forced to admit to about 20 toxic effects.
- rBGH milk is contaminated by pus, due to the mastitis commonly induced by rBGH, and antibiotics used to treat the mastitis.
- rBGH milk is chemically and nutritionally different than natural milk.
- rBGH milk is contaminated with rBGH, traces of which are absorbed in the gut.
- rBGH is supercharged with high levels of a natural growth factor (IGF-1), which is readily absorbed into the gut.
- Excess levels of IGF-1 have been incriminated as a cause of breast, colon, and prostate cancers. IGF-1 blocks natural defense mechanisms against early submicroscopic cancers.

- rBGH factory farms pose a major threat to the viability of small dairy farms.
- **rBGH enriches Monsanto**, while posing dangers, without any benefits to consumers, especially in view of the current national surplus of milk.

The risks of cancer to consumers, particularly their children, who are enrolled in the Public School Lunch Program, are indisputable. Please refer to the Web site for a list of the top rBGH & rBGH-Free Processors (2006). *www.organicconsumers.org/rBGH/rbghlist.csfm*

Few are aware that 95% of all serotonin production in the body lies not in the brain but in the gut. The gut, in fact, has even more neurons than the brain! The brain and the gut are inextricably linked.
—Nora Gedgaudas, *Primal Body—Primal Mind*

Food for Thought— Daily Protein Requirements

For you to understand the *sustainable eating plan* please know that I followed the guidelines for daily protein requirements that Nora Gedgaudas recommends in her book *Primal Body—Primal Mind*. The total protein requirement for the entire day (the approximate RDA) is between 45–55 grams per adult, maybe a little more for extremely active individuals. You will see that the amount of meat, chicken, and fish in each recipe seems unusually low. This is correct, however. It is important *not to overeat protein*. **Protein, when consumed in excess, converts to sugar**. This is an important fact to know. You're body and brain only require a few ounces of nutrient dense protein per meal to function at optimum levels. What you are also going to realize, and this is a **Big Point** I want to bring home, eating these *smaller amounts* of nutrient dense, "complete" proteins are going to make a huge difference in your family food budget. *Better nutrition and economy*. What a deal!

It's also very important to know how essential proper amounts of good dietary fats are for your metabolism and the regulation of your entire hormonal balance. Ms. Gedgaudes is unequivocal in stating, "The more that dietary fat serves as your primary source of fuel and not carbohydrate, the better you will become at fat burning and the healthier and slimmer, you will ultimately be . . . AND the longer you will live. It turns out, in fact, that the very thing we have been told is our worst possible enemy actually may be our very best friend, if not our salvation."

With this understanding in mind I have included only the recommended dietary fats in all the recipes in this book (see the pantry section on oils). Dietary fat in the appropriate amounts will sustain your energy much longer. It is unlikely that you will experience discomfort or cravings once you adjust to the sustainable diet. Good fats keep hormones in balance, keep insulin down, and help us stay feeling satisfied longer. You are much less likely to get grumpy and irritable, experience mood swings and anxiety and general brain fog if you are eating good fats (oils) with each meal.

According to Ms. Gedgaudas,

High protein diets are not advisable or necessary to be healthy and slim and can lead to numerous problems. The trick is in maximizing the quality of the source, digestibility of the protein, and/or quality of your digestion—and what you combine it with, so that you can make the most out of this precious commodity.

Digestion takes more energy to perform than any other daily human activity. Eating more optimally sufficient amounts of *complete protein*—particularly when not over-cooked or combined with starches—actually greatly helps improve your digestion and assimilation of it, and you will expend much less energy doing so . . . which you will have for other things! ***In fact, you may be utterly shocked to discover how much energy it is possible for you to have.***

With the following table you will be able to determine the quantity of protein you want to have at each meal. This would also include protein from incomplete and plant sources of protein. You can see how much of the non-starchy vegetables you can eat with your meals. Eating the vegetables with the protein and the good fats will make you feel full longer.

Appendix G, Page 345, *Primal Body—Primal Mind*

Sources: USDA Nutrient Database for Standard Reference.
Complete Sources (note that amount of protein varies with fat content.
More fat=less protein per serving). The following are approximations.

Based on a 3 ounce serving:
▶ Eggs (medium): 6 grams
▶ Fish (3 oz): 21 grams
▶ Cheese (cheddar): 25 grams
▶ Roast beef: 28 grams
▶ Roast chicken: 25 grams
▶ Other meats (avg): 25 grams
▶ Sausages: 12 grams
▶ Ham: 18 grams
▶ Beef burgers: 20 grams
▶ Corned beef: 26 grams
▶ Liver: 23 grams
▶ Sirloin steak: 24
▶ Turkey: 25 grams
▶ Shrimp: 18–21 grams
▶ Tuna: 22 grams
▶ Ground beef (regular): 23 grams
▶ Ground beef (lean): 24 grams
▶ Spareribs (lean): 22 grams
▶ Chicken breast: 25 grams
▶ Lobster: 17 grams
▶ Salmon: 22 grams
▶ Feta cheese: 12 grams
▶ Duck (roasted): 24 grams
▶ Whole milk yogurt (8 oz): 7 grams

Protein Content in Incomplete or Plant Sources of Foods:

▶ Nuts (walnuts, Brazil nuts) ¼ cup: 5 grams
▶ Cashews (¼ cup): 5 grams
▶ Peanuts (¼ cup): 9.5 grams
▶ Peanut butter (2 tbs): 8 grams
▶ Almonds (¼ cup): 7.5 grams
▶ Pine nuts (¼ cup): 7.5 grams
▶ Sunflower seeds (¼ cup): 6.5 grams
▶ Oatmeal (1 cup): 6 grams
▶ Black beans (¼ cup): 4.5 grams
▶ Pinto beans (¼ cup): 3.5 grams
▶ Chick peas (¼ cup): 4 grams
▶ Hummus: 5 grams
▶ Tabbouli: (3 oz) 3 grams
▶ Quinoa (½ cup): 4.5 grams
▶ Lentils (½ cup): 9 grams
▶ Tempeh (½ cup): 20 grams
▶ Brown rice (½ cup): 2.5 grams
▶ Stir-fried vegetables (½ cup): 2 grams
▶ Broccoli (½ cup): 2.5–3 grams
▶ Spinach (½ cup): 2.5 grams
▶ Coconut milk (1 cup): 6 grams

A Word About Produce

Few human endeavors have as much impact on our planet as the cultivation of food. It is essential at this time in our history that we do not compromise our food sources and our water, soils, and air. Chemicals wind up in our groundwater, rivers, and deltas. They wind up in our food, bodies, and breast milk. Almost a half million farm workers are poisoned by exposure to pesticides every year.

When you go to the grocery store and see one stack of red tomatoes next to another stack of red tomatoes labeled "organic," and before you choose the cheaper tomatoes, consider how they are grown. Conventional tomatoes begin life in a greenhouse usually in a *synthetic starter* fertilizer. At a certain point the tomatoes are moved to a field that has been treated with 400–600 pounds per acre of additional chemical fertilizers. Many tomato plants are also sprayed with fungicides, which are highly toxic to fish and birds.

The organic method of tomato growing goes something like this: In the fall the land usually gets some kind of cover crop to provide nutrients and organic matter to the soil. The young tomato plants are started in a greenhouse using a mixture of compost, peat moss, fish emulsion, and seaweed extract (sounds good enough to eat). Ladybugs are used to eat the aphids. Composted chicken manure, limestone, and potash are used instead of a chemical fertilizer. After planting the tomatoes in the ground, the beds are then covered with straw mulch to keep down the weeds. When you buy organic produce you are buying a whole farming system that is more labor intensive and not harmful to the environment. Wouldn't you pay a little more for that peace of mind and contribution to our precious planet? Remember that the cost of buying organic foods may be more, but you will no longer be buying *"expensive"* and environmentally unsustainable, pre-packaged foods, beverages, pastries, ice cream, and bottled salad dressings. The trade off is worth it.

NATURAL GRASS FED — **PINE MOUNTAIN RANCH** — **BUFFALO YAK · ELK**

USDA
Bend Oregon

Local Grown On Grass Alone

EXOTIC MEATS
www.pmrbuffalo.com

GRASS FED BEEF
SALE REG $4.99

BEEF GROUND	$4.99 lb
BEEF RIB EYE	$16.99 lb
BEEF T-BONE	$13.99 lb
CHATEAUBRIAND	$10.99 lb
BEEF FLAT IRON	$9.99 lb
SIRLOIN TIP	$8.99 lb
BEEF ROUND/CHUCK/CUBE	$5.99 lb
BEEF SHORT RIBS	$4.99 lb
BEEF TENDERLOIN	$26.99 lb
1/3lb STEAK BURGER PATTIES (5 PACK)	$10.00 Pack
PORTERHOUSE	$16.99
BEEF FLANK	$13.99 lb

BUFFALO MEAT (GRASS ONLY)

Buffalo Filet Mignon	$14.98 8oz / $29.95 lb
Buffalo New York	$9.99 8oz / $19.99 lb
Buffalo Rib Eye	$9.99 8oz / $19.99 lb
Buffalo Chateaubriand	$15.99 lb
Buffalo Flat Iron	$12.99 lb
Buffalo Top Sirloin	$7.35 8oz / $14.99 lb
Buffalo Skirt Steak	$5.65 8oz / $11.99 lb
Buffalo Sirloin Tip	$11.99 lb
Buffalo Chuck / Stew meat Round / Cube	$9.99 lb
Buffalo Steak Patties 1/3lb 5 pack	$16.00
BUFFALO GROUND	$7.99 lb
YAK OR ELK GROUND	$9.99 lb
Buffalo Short Ribs	$6.99 lb
Buffalo Heart or Liver	$4.29 lb
Buffalo Back Ribs	$4.99 lb

Buffalo Tongue	$7.99 lb
Buffalo Kabob	$11.99 lb
Buffalo Sweet Italian	$10.99 lb
Buffalo Brat Links	$12.99 lb
Buffalo Breakfast Saus	$9.99 lb
North Country Links	$11.99 lb
All Natural Buf Country Links	$11.99 lb
Buffalo Summer Sausage	$14.99 lb
Buffalo Pepperoni	$10.99 pack
Buffalo Jerky	$10.00 Pack 2 ea
Buffalo Oxtail	$4.99 lb
Buffalo Rocky Mountain Oysters (pairs only)	$3.99 lb
Buffalo Stock Bones or Dog Treats	$2.29 lb

on sale! $1.50 lb

Let's Go Shopping

It's best to do your major shopping once a week when you have the time to pay attention. Make a master list that has all the ingredients you will be using so you can run a copy off from your computer as needed. Keep it handy as a reminder and check things off during the week that you will need. This way you will have your list ready. I have made a suggested list for your pantry, but it's up to you to select the ones that will become your favorites. You may want to form or join a food co-op and buy in bulk (Organic Azure Foods, Oregon) or buy grass-fed meat directly from the producers and freeze it. This could add up to tremendous yearly savings on your food budget. Buying in bulk also saves the environment and the waste of those small packages we are constantly recycling.

Your Nearest Farmer's Market

One place you might want to begin shopping, if you haven't already, is your local farmers market. This is the best way to get acquainted with the regional growers of organic fruits and vegetables in your area. There will also be local producers of cheese, *pastured* poultry, eggs, and grass-fed meats. The farmer's market is a wonderful place to learn about selecting, preparing, and preserving the bounty of your region. The farmer's market makes a great educational Saturday event for the kids. Let them have the fun of picking out the food for the week and tasting some treats.

Who shops at Farmer's Markets? According to the Portland Farmer's Market survey:

- 75% women and 38% of our shoppers have an annual income over $60,000
- Avid cooks, restaurant goers, and gardeners
- People who are vitally interested in health and nutrition
- Widely varied in age, with 70% in the 25–54 age group

- Nearly 80% are college graduates (35% with post-graduate or professional degrees)
- Active seniors who have the time and income for farmer's market shopping
- Families with children who combine shopping with education about nutrition and farming
- Lower-income families and seniors who benefit from the Farm Direct Nutrition. Programs for Women, Infants & Children (WIC) and low-income seniors; and Oregon Trail EBT customers.

Find a farmers market in your state. The National Directory of Farmer's Markets guidebook is published annually by the USDA. *www.ams.gov/farmersmarkets*

One reason to go to the farmer's market

Few are aware that omega-3 fatty acids—known also as alpha-linolenic acid, EPA, and DHA—are easily the single most deficient nutrient in the modern Western diet. Insufficient intake of this vital and essential dietary component is linked with virtually every modern disease process, weight problem, affective disorder, and learning disability.
—Nora Gedgaudas, *Primal Body—Primal Mind*

Your Pantry

Love: The most important ingredient for your pantry is love. Be sure to keep a lot of it on hand. It is our love of cooking and feeding our families and ourselves that is the true nourishment. Our bodies know when food is lovingly prepared and love is the real fuel that helps us meet all of life's wonders and predicaments well.

Green Foods are perhaps the most healing foods on the planet and probably the single most important addition you can make to any sustainable eating plan. You can experiment with various brands, but three that I recommend are Pure Synergy, The Ultimate Superfood Formula, ordered from Dr. Ron's Ultra Pure, *www.DrRon.com*, NanoGreens, and Vitamineral Green. They contain a full spectrum of naturally occurring, absorbable and non-toxic vitamins and minerals, all the essential amino acids (protein) antioxidants, chlorophyll, soluble and non-soluble fibers, and tens of thousands of phytonutrients. Go to the Raw Food World Web site. *www.rawfoodworld.com*. You can also order the Vitamineral Green on Amazon. For NanoGreens go to *www.nanogreens.com*.

Dietary Fats

An important paper to read is "The Oiling of America" by Sally Fallon, M.A., the author of *Nourishing Traditions: The Cookbook that Challenges Politically Correct Nutrition and the Diet Dictocrates.* In the article Ms. Fallon documents the politics behind the cholesterol theory of heart disease. She also gives a detailed description of what fats and oils are good for us and why. *www.westonprice.org/knowyourfats/oilinghtml*

Using the following "good" fats in our diet is necessary for weight loss. When you eat a combination of good fats throughout the day, and in sufficient quantities, your cravings for carbohydrates will diminish and your blood sugar will remain stable. With good fats your body will remain satisfied longer, hunger pangs will disappear and eating sensibly will become the norm.

Oils (fats): A good fat is a traditional fat like butter from cows eating grass, natural animal fat, and cold pressed traditional oils like coconut oil, sesame oil, palm oil, olive oil, and flax oil. (Flax oil is not a cooking oil, however). Good oils contain essential fatty acids, omega 3, 6 & 9 and are necessary in the diet to maintain optimum health. **The ratio of omega-3 to omega-6 in our diet should be no more than 1:4 (one part omega-3 to 4 parts omega-6). A 1:1 ratio is optimum.** Fatty acids are strong antioxidants, they help boost the immune system and actually help the body burn excess fat. Cooked oils cannot be broken down easily by the body and so they promote weight gain and may lead to many health problems. The best way to avoid a diet cooked with fat is to not eat foods that are fried in a lot of oil. Good oils, like the ones listed below, should be the only ones you use when preparing food. Since oils are high in calories, you will need to determine the correct amount of daily oils that are just right in your diet.

Pasture Fed Butter: Butter from *pastured* (grass-fed) cows is rich in short and medium chain fatty acids, including even small amounts of lauric acid. Because grass is richer in vitamin E, A, and beta-carotine than stored hay or standard dairy diets, butter from dairy cows grazing on fresh pasture is also richer in these important nutrients. You can use *pastured* butter more liberally in your diet. *www.grassfedtraditions.com* or *www.organicpastures.com*.

Olive Oil Education: Olive oil is healthy for you and it's delicious. Not all olive oils are the same however. Please visit the California Estate Olive Oil and Market, *www.caloliveoil.com.* They specialize in rare, small batch, locally grown and fresh California Olive Oils. The following information was permitted to use from their Web site.

What does it mean when an olive oil is certified by the California Olive Oil Council? To guarantee consumer confidence in California Extra Virgin Olive Oil, the California Olive Oil Council (COOC) introduced its "Seal of Quality" program in 1998. Only 100% California Extra Virgin Olive Oils without defects can display the seal. To be considered for certification, olive growers must submit their oil(s) to the COOC Panel of Tasters for sensory evaluation and have a chemical analysis conducted. The chemical analysis determines if the oil contains 0.5% (or less) free fatty acids as well as a peroxide value of 20 meq 02/kg or less. The COOC Panel of Tasters has undertaken a training and certification program. The team meets each month for the dual purpose of selecting oils for the COOC program as well as for continual training.

Why do hand picked olives produce a more superior olive oil? The best method for olive harvesting is by hand. Olives tend to bruise when allowed to drop on the ground. Bruised olives may ferment and oxidize, which leads to an inferior quality of oil. Of course, hand harvesting is labor intensive. The reason such care is necessary is because hand picked olives produce a pure oil . . . an "extra virgin" oil.

What are some of the general terms to use when describing aromas and tastes found in Certified California Extra Virgin Olive Oils? Here are some common aromas and tastes: nutty, almond, grassy, fruity, floral, peppery, chili peppers, tomato, artichoke, apple, olives, butter, and caramel.

Why do imported oils and discounted/inexpensive oils from the grocery store not have the above tastes even though they are labeled extra virgin? Keep in mind that imported oils arrive months to years after production. Other oils that have sat on a grocery store shelf, been discounted, or are exposed to bright light and heat lose their freshness (olive oil is perishable). They are more likely to taste rancid, bitter, metallic, musty, or smell fermented.

California has become just as famous for its wonderful olive oils as it has for its award winning wines. In California olive oil, like fine wine, can be produced in different varieties. The five commonly grown olives are Arbequena, Ascalano, Frantoio, Manzanillo, and Mission. The oils come from groves in northern and central California. Some of the producers of premium olive oils are: Bava Family Grove, (Colline de Santa Cruz), Carriage Vineyards (Arbequena and Manzanillo Extra Virgin Olive Oil), Olivina Mission (Extra Virgin Unfiltered Olive Oil), McEvoy Ranch (Organic Extra Virgin Olive Oil), Lucero Flavored Olive Oils (great as a finishing oil), Robbins Family Farm Tuscan Blend, and B.R. Cohn, just to name a few. Bariani Stone crushed organic olive oil is fabulous.

Nut Oils: Nut oils can really spruce up your salads, vegetables, and seafood. Just a little of the oil is drizzled on food for a truly wonderful taste sensation. One of the world's most famous producers of artisan nut oil is J LeBlanc from Burgundy, France. This company has been in the nut oil business for 130 years. J Le Blanc makes the oils in small batches and the result is the oil tastes exactly like the nuts they are made from.

The J Le Blanc nuts oils are Almond, Grilled Peanut, Grilled Sesame, Walnut, Pumpkinseed, Hazelnut, Pecan, and Pistachio. You can purchase them by going to *www.klkellerimports.com.*

Organic Unrefined *Virgin* Coconut Oil and Coconut Butter: Virgin coconut oil has been used to cook with since ancient times. It has been used in the Ayervedic medicine of India and has long been advocated for its therapeutic qualities. Coconut oil contains no trans-fatty acids. As a cooking oil, its chemical structure is kept intact and is therefore resistant to mutation of fatty acid chains even at high temperatures so it makes a superb cooking oil. Research shows that the medium chain fatty acids found in coconut oil boost the body's metabolism, raises body temperature and helps to provide energy necessary for weight loss. Coconut oil provides *satiation,* which is necessary for weight loss. If you use coconut oil on a consistent basis you provide vital nourishment to every cell of your body. Virgin coconut oil is rich in lauric acid (found in mother's breast milk), a nutrient that supports the immune system. Lauric acid is also an antiviral and antifungal. *Virgin* coconut oil means that the oil has been extracted by a method that does not involve high heat and harmful chemicals. *Most commercial coconut oil is refined, bleached and deodorized, so make sure to read the label and make sure it is virgin coconut oil that you are buying.*

Palm Kernel Oil: Palm oil is extracted from the seed of the palm fruit, which is very oily and is widely consumed in Africa and Asia. Some European food manufacturers are now using it in their baked food products and snack foods. Palm oil is also high in lauric acid.

Organic Unrefined Sesame Oil: People have been consuming sesame oil for over 5000 years. During the 1930s sesame oil was in wide use in the United States and we were importing huge amounts of sesame seeds every year. After World War II the use of *inexpensive soybean and cottonseed oils* became prevalent. Sesame oil is trans-fat free and contains sesamol and sesamin, natural antioxidants found in both the oil and the seeds. Sesame oil is an essential ingredient in Asian cooking and is adaptable to all kinds of cooking. Extra virgin, expeller pressed, sesame oil is available from Eden Foods. *www.edenfoods.com.* Loriva

Extra Virgin Sesame Oil is another domestic cold-pressed oil available at many gourmet markets.

Ghee—"better than butter": I use ghee in my cooking and love it. It has a wonderful buttery flavor. Ghee is *clarified* butter. The butter is slowly simmered in a saucepan over low heat until three layers form. The top layer is foamy and will be skimmed off. The middle, liquid gold layer is the ghee. The milk solids layer sinks to the bottom of the pan. After the ghee is clear I strain it through a fine sieve or cheesecloth.

Ghee will not burn while sautéing, it has a very high smoke point and its chemical structure does not change at high heat. Since all the milk proteins have been removed during the clarifying process, it is lactose free, which means it can be used in recipes that call for butter. Ghee, made from grass-fed butter, is nutrient dense and contains CLA, fat soluble vitamins, A, D, E, and K2 (activator X). In 1945, Dr. Weston A. Price described what he called "Activator X" as a critical nutrient for optimal health. This "X Factor" has now been identified as Vitamin K-2. This vitamin is naturally occurring in the fat of ruminants that graze upon green grass.

To make ghee: simmer 1 pound *pasture-fed* (KerryGold), or another brand of pastured butter, for about twenty minutes. Skim foam as necessary. When clarified, strain and store in jars. Divide the ghee into several small jars. Keep one near the stove for cooking (it does not need refrigeration) and the remaining ghee in the refrigerator for future use.

Goose and Duck Fat: You can buy duck and goose fat but it is expensive and may be a little hard to find. Duck and goose fat come in cans and can usually be found at your local gourmet market. These rendered fats are delicious and can be used for sautéing.

Pig's Lard: It is difficult to find pig's lard that comes from pastured pigs (without preservatives), therefore I have not included its use in the recipes in this book. For locally produced lard from pastured pigs you might try contacting your local chapter of the Weston A. Price Foundation, *westonprice.org*. You can also check the classified ads in *Wise Traditions*, the foundation's quarterly magazine.

The single most potent trigger of hormonal dysregulation is chronic carbohydrate consumption and subsequent blood sugar surges.
—Nora Gedgaudas, *Primal Body—Primal Mind*

Gluten-Free Grains

Quinoa is technically a seed, not a grain, and is related to spinach, beets, and Swiss chard. To the Incas of pre-Columbian Peru, quinoa was revered as the "Mother Grain." It has been hailed recently as today's top secret, super food. Those who cannot tolerate gluten will be happy to know the American Celiac Spru Association lists quinoa as "consistent with a gluten-free diet." Quinoa's natural sapotin coating must be removed by soaking and rinsing before cooking. However, Eden Foods brand organic quinoa has had the sapotin coating mechanically removed by rubbing. Organic quinoa is now available at most grocery stores. You can get it in big bags at Costco, very reasonably priced.

Forbidden Rice imported by Lotus Foods is an unusual and delicious deep purple rice. Originally grown for royalty, this heirloom rice is available for all to enjoy. Use Forbidden Rice for a special occasion. You can probably find this rice at a good gourmet grocery. Check the Lotus Foods Web site for all their top quality rice varietals. *www.lotusfoods.com.*

Purple Jasmine Rice, from Phakao cooperative, in Thailand and Ruby Jasmine Rice, from Surin cooperative in Thailand, are unique. Imported by Alter Eco, they are Fair Trade certified. *www.fairtradecertified.org.* Also, check out *www.altereco.com* for their other Fair Trade products.

American Wild Rice: Although wild rice is grown commercially in the U.S. there is a brand of wild rice from Nett Lake in northern Minnesota, located on the Boise Forte Indian Reservation. Due to its remote location, near the top of three major American watersheds, this lake is naturally isolated from sources of pollution. The Boise Forte Band allows no fertilizers, pesticides, or outboard motors on the lake. The wild rice from Nett Lake is hand harvested in the traditional way by two persons in a canoe. The green rice is then roasted over a wood fire to remove moisture. Wild rice is rich in essential vitamins and minerals. To purchase this special American product go to *www.netlakewildrice. com.* Oregon and California are producers of wild rice as well. *www. oregonwildrice.com*

Tellicherri Peppercorns come from India. Freshly ground pepper makes all the difference in cooking. Get a good pepper grinder and keep it handy.

Celtic Sea Salt from one of the most pristine coastal regions of France is the recommended sea salt to use. It is harvested by a method, which preserves its purity and the balance of ocean minerals. Celtic sea salt contains higher levels of minerals and trace elements than all the other sea salts. Try the Flower of the Ocean finishing salt. *www. celticseasalt.com.*

Himalayan Pink Salt is hand mined. This ancient sea salt is harvested from the foothills of the Himalayas and is unrefined and unpolluted. It is approximately 250 million years old and is one of the purest salts in the world. It is reported to contain 84 trace elements.

Redmond RealSalt is an unrefined and pure sea salt from an ancient sea bed in Utah. Near the small town of Redmond, Utah, this beautifully pink salt is extracted from deep within the earth. Redmond RealSalt is not bleached, kiln dried, heated or altered with pollutants. Is also has a full complement of trace minerals. It is reasonably priced and readily available at most groceries.

Vinegars: Acidity is what makes a vinegar stand out. A great vinegar imparts fruitiness, fragrance, and depth to a dish. You might want to try an American Balsamic from New Mexico, *Traditional Aceto Balsamico* of Monticello, or *Datu Puti Coconut Vinegar* from the Philippines, *Gold Plum Chinkaing Vinegar* from China or an unfiltered, unpasteurized apple cider vinegar from Quebec, *Verger Pierre Gingras Natural Handcrafted Cider Vinegar.* I use *Bragg's Raw Unfiltered Organic Apple Cider Vinegar* at home. I also can't live without *Marukan Seasoned Rice Wine Vinegar.*

Miso: It is very important to use a miso that is un-pasteurized, organic and GMO-free. Most of us are familiar with the red and white miso. Miso is available at most health foods stores and gourmet groceries.

Raw Nuts and Seeds: Nuts and seeds are a good additional source of protein and essential fatty acids in the diet. Keep your pantry well stocked with *"raw"* organic almonds, cashews, sunflower seeds, pumpkin seeds, chia seeds, sesame and flax seeds, walnuts, pine nuts, pecans, hazelnuts, and Brazil nuts. Please visit the Braga Organic Farms Web site for a selection bulk organic almonds, pistachios, walnuts, and dried organic cranberries. *Buyorganicnuts.com.* D&S Ranches in California also carries organic nuts. *www.california-almonds.com.* D&S carries bulk almonds, walnuts, pistachios, and pecans. D&S Ranch has developed a safe steam (non-pasteurized) method for removing bacteria from their almonds before shipping. This method still allows them to sell their almonds as "raw," therefore preserving the internal natural balance of enzymes, amino acids, and proteins. You can actually sprout these almonds.

Oregon produces hazelnuts. I located Freddy Guys Hazelnuts at the Portland Farmer's Market. *www.freddyguys.com.* Golden Omega Flax Seed from Heavenly Harvest in Corvallis, Oregon is a pesticide free flax seed.

Soaking the seeds and nuts in *salted* water is an important step, which will eliminate phytates and tripsin inhibitors. The exception would be Brazil nuts or hazelnuts, as they contain no enzyme inhibitors. Soaking begins the sprouting process so that all the important nutrition is made available. A general rule of thumb for soaking is:

almonds, 12 hours	cashews, 8 hours
flax seeds, 8 hours	pecans, 2 hours
pumpkinseeds, 4–6 hours	walnuts, 2 hours
sunflower seeds, 4–6 hours	

Rinse the seeds and nuts well after soaking then dry on a sheetpan in a 150 degree oven.

Dairy: Milk from *grass-fed* cows has a much higher content of omega-3 fatty acids. The omega-3 fatty acids in most conventional dairy products today are very low, and most people are dangerously deficient in them. Almost all dairy cows today (85–95%) are raised in confinement on a diet of grain, mostly corn. This is the agribusiness method because it's efficient and cost effective. The grain based diet causes ph changes in the cows and increases the need for the use of antibiotics. The result is that the omega-3 fatty acids in grain fed cows is very low and the omega-6 fatty acids, of which most people are consuming too many these days, is high. Grass-fed cows and cows milk is higher in conjugated linolenic acid (CLA). It is a naturally occurring free fatty acid found in meat and dairy products. The most abundant source of natural CLA is the meat and dairy products of grass-fed animals. In addition raw dairy products contain the Wulzen factor, also known as the "anti-stiffness" factor, beneficial for healthy joints. Go to the Campaign for Real Milk Web site *www.RealMilk.org.*

Low-Fat Dairy products (skim milk, 1% and 2%) are made up mainly of carbohydrates and should be avoided. The low fat milks also contain large amounts of oxidized cholesterol. *Heavy cream has no carbohydrates.*

Non-Dairy Milks: Nut milks and coconut milk are good substitutes for those who cannot have dairy. You can even make your own nut milks by soaking the nuts overnight in filtered water. Puree the nuts in the blender with additional water and then strain the nut milk through a nut milk bag or cheesecloth. It's better to make your own as some of the commercial nut milks are sweetened with cane juice and have high sugar content. I've included a recipe for making almond milk. It's much richer and creamier than store bought.

Coconut Ice Cream: I am happy to report that coconut ice cream is a spectacular alternative to ice cream and it beats, hands down, soy ice creams and rice ice creams that taste disappointing to say the least. I have included recipes in the dessert section for coconut ice creams.

Sugar Substitutes: I recommend *Stevita* stevia, one of the purest stevia products on the market (with 95% steviosides). Stevita has no fillers or other harmful ingredients like some other stevia products. It also comes in flavors like Chocolate, Cognac, Mango, Orange, Peach, Peppermint, Strawberry, and Toffee. Stevia is a non-carbohydrate, non-caloric sweetener that can be used by those who cannot tolerate sugar or other sweeteners. I recommended using stevia *to taste* in many of the recipes that call for a sweetener. Stevita stevia is cultivated in one of the best and richest soils in the world (the southern Brazilian red clay soil) by Steviafarma, which is a company conscientious of the preservation of the environment and continuously searching for social harmony through spiritual, ecological, and sustainable industrial farming practices. *www.stevitastevia.com*. Order from VitaCost, *www.vitacost.com* or *www.MyVitanet.com*.

Fresh Herbs: Fresh herbs make all the difference in the flavor of a dish. If you don't have a garden you can have some herbs in pots in the kitchen window. Favorite herbs to grow would be sage, rosemary, marjoram, oregano, and a variety of thyme and various mints. If you live in a region where you can grow your own basil, then grow as much as you can to make pesto to freeze for use during the year. You can never have enough basil.

Fresh Ginger: I keep my ginger frozen and just take it out, as needed. Use a microplane grater and you will see the difference it makes. Put the ginger immediately back in the freezer.

The Grass-Fed Movement

The good news is that since the late '90s a growing number of ranchers have stopped fattening their animals on grain such as genetically modified soy, corn, and other supplements. Now they allow the animals to roam free and eat pasture grass. The pastured animals are healthier and do not require hormones and antibiotics to stave off disease and they are allowed to lead a stress free life. When it comes time to kill these animals it is also done in a very humane way so the animals do not suffer. When cattle are taken to feed lots and finished on grains they lose the essential omega-3 fatty acids which change to omega-6. We now have an overabundance of omega-6 in our American diet. It is important to know that the ideal ratio of omega-3 fatty acids to omega-6 is 1:1, and should be no more than 1:4. Also, vitamins and minerals are cancelled out in grain-fed animals. These are only some of the reasons to buy grass-fed meats, poultry, and dairy.

The meat and dairy products from grass-fed animals, (beef, bison, lamb, and goats) retain the health-promoting fats such as omega-3s and "conjugated linolenic acid," or CLA. Conjugated linolenic acid may be one of our most potent defenses against cancer. Omega-3 fatty acids are most abundant in seafood, but they are also found in animals raised on pasture. The meat is leaner and has less harmful fats and is therefore lower in overall calories. Meat, eggs, and dairy from pastured animals are richer in antioxidants: including vitamin E, beta-carotene, and vitamin C. Switching to grass-fed meat and dairy products is one way to restore these precious nutrients to your diet.

Pastured chickens, which are raised outdoors and allowed to eat bugs and spend time in the sunshine, also have higher levels of essential nutrients in their meat and eggs. They have up to six times the levels of vitamin D, another essential vitamin missing from our American diet. In fact vitamin D may be the most important vitamin for our overall health. It is estimated that eating just two eggs from pastured chickens will give you 63–126% of the recommended daily intake of vitamin D. Be careful when the reading label on your egg carton. Just because the carton says "certified" organic, free-range or fed an "all-vegetarian diet," is no guarantee they were pastured. Look for pastured eggs in your market and ask the grocer to carry these. Be diligent. Better yet purchase the eggs at the farmers market.

For a comprehensive Web site on the benefits of grass-fed products and how to locate suppliers in your state, please go to Eat Wild, *www.eatwild.com.*

GRASS FED BEEF

Always Naturally Raised With

- No Antibiotics
- No Added Hormones
- No Animal By Products

IT'S WHAT'S FOR DINNER.®

PASTURE RAISED LAMB

Always Naturally Raised With

- No Sub-therapeutic Antibiotics
- No Added Hormones
- No Animal By Products

AMERICAN LAMB
FRESH HOMEGROWN FLAVOR

The Power of Community
How Cuba Survived Peak Oil

This past year I bought the film *The Power of Community: How Cuba Survived Peak Oil.* It is one of the most inspiring and positive films I have ever seen, and I highly recommend watching it as a family or with your neighbors. It shows, graphically and wonderfully, how an entire nation came together under extreme hardship and threat of starvation to actually create a better, healthier lifestyle than they had before they lost the source of oil, which ran their country.

When the Soviet Union collapsed in 1990, Cuba's economy went into a tailspin. With imports of oil cut by more than half—and food by 80%—people were desperate. This film tells of the hardships and struggles as well as the community and creativity of the Cuban people during this difficult time. Cubans share how they transitioned from a highly mechanized, industrial agricultural system to one using organic methods of farming and local, urban gardens. It is an unusual look into the Cuban culture during this economic crisis, which they call, "The Special Period." The film opens with a short history of Peak Oil, a term for the time in our history when world oil production will reach its all-time peak and begin to decline forever *(this peak was reached in the 1970s)*. Cuba, the only country that has faced such a crisis— the massive reduction of fossil fuels—is an example of options and hope. Visit *www.communitysolutions.org.*

Even though the United States has not experienced the sudden withdrawal of our oil supply, which is a possibility to consider, there are lessons to be learned from this film. We are now in an *economic crisis* that is becoming global. The *transportation* of food drives up the costs of food, and everything else, to the consumer. The longer the distance food has to be shipped, the more oil is used to get it to its destination. We can no longer as a nation continue to overlook this fact. This film shows what communities can do to work together to produce their own food and to produce food that is healthier through organic farming methods. It is really time to think about community and teaching ourselves and our children how to survive and *thrive* in tough economic times.

A public that better understands the state of the world's oceans can be a driving force in helping governments pass laws to ban destructive fishing practices.

Turning the Tide

This article is reprinted with permission from the Blue Ocean Institute Web site and I felt it was important to include in the book so we can continue to pay attention to preserving our oceans, the source of seafood for the coming generations.

In a 2006 study published in the journal *Science* an international group of ecologists and economists concluded that loss of biodiversity is profoundly reducing the ocean's ability to produce seafood, resist disease, filter pollutants, and rebound from stresses such as overfishing and climate change. This study led to headlines around the world hailing, "the end of seafood by 2048."

However, as the lead author noted at the time, "this is not a prediction. It's a *possible* outcome based on a projection of existing data." The study also strikes a note of hope by recognizing the inherent ability of ocean ecosystems to self-heal and regenerate, under the right circumstances. In other words, it is not too late for the ocean and fisheries.

All seafood buyers can influence this outcome through their buying choices—and many already are. All those involved in the seafood value chain—from fishermen to retailer to consumer—have a responsibility to ensure a lasting and diverse supply of seafood for generations to come.

The Role of Seafood Choices Alliance

Founded in 2001, *Seafood Choices Alliance* is an international association advancing the market for sustainable seafood. The Alliance helps the seafood industry—from fishermen and fish farmers to distributors, wholesalers, retailers, and restaurants—make the seafood marketplace environmentally, economically, and socially sustainable. Seafood Choices Alliance convenes and connects the world's leading voices in support of a sustainable supply of seafood choices, highlighting the need for a global solution to threats facing the ocean. Seafood Choices Alliance is a partnership-based association that invites and challenges corporations to engage in more responsible behavior and leverages the collective power of key players to drive change across the seafood marketplace.

Consumer Responsibility

Consumers are becoming more active in choosing sustainability at the counter and at the table. In the United States, the most recognizable tool for consumers is the *wallet card of seafood recommendations.* Wallet cards offer consumers a very basic picture of sustainability, generally categorized in a traffic light system of "green" for best choices, "yellow" for good options, and "red" for seafood items to avoid. Cards have been developed by a number of conservation organizations in the United States, including Blue Ocean Institute, Environmental Defense Fund, and Monterey Bay Aquarium's Seafood Watch Program.

Another tool, just developed for consumers is *Blue Ocean Institute's Fish Phone*, a sustainable seafood text messaging service. Now consumers with a question about seafood sustainability send a text message with the name of the fish in question and rapidly get a response with assessment information and better alternatives for fish with environmental concerns.

I highly recommend going to the Blue Ocean Institute Web site for everything you need to know about seafood choices. It's a beautiful Web site. Also, please go to the *Science* magazine's Web site and look up an article titled "Oceans Without Fish."

LINDA BRAND CRAB
SEAFOOD
CHINOOK WA
"SHIP TO SHORE FRESH TO YOUR DOOR"

Breakfast For Two

We went out to dinner
Boy, what an appetite
We just couldn't stop eating
We stayed up most of the night

And after three or four hours
Stomachs began to hurt
But everythin' tasted so good
We didn't stop until after dessert

Ooh-la-la breakfast for two
Ooh-la-la, you got me, yes, and I got you

I've eaten in Italy
Yes, I've eaten in Spain
I must admit I'd be lickin' my lips
If I ever was to eat there again

But last night at dinner
You really blew my mind
The way we supped just filled me up
I think about food all of the time

People always come up to me
They say, hey man, how 'bout a little smile
don't take life so seriously
Lighten up for a little while

I say that a man's a fool
If he don't know how to cry
When I get down I do get down
But when I'm up I know how to fly

Cuisine for Whole Health

Reprinted with permission, Country Joe McDonald, Alkatraz Music

A Good Breakfast

The human body is capable of great strength, endurance and longevity given proper nutrition.
—Diana Schwarzbein, MD, *The Schwarzbein Principle*

Some things bear repeating. Children need a good breakfast of protein and good fats for their developing brains. Children do not have to be overweight. Remember diet effects mood and will, in turn, affect behavior. So let's have a good sustainable breakfast to begin the day. If you begin the day with a breakfast of 2–3 ounces of meat, or eggs and vegetables prepared with butter from grass-fed cows your body will not need to make extra cholesterol.

"When you restrict dietary cholesterol and force the body to make its own cholesterol, your body will make more cholesterol than it needs. But if you eat a meal that does not contain cholesterol, such as a breakfast of skim milk, fruit, and orange juice, your body overproduces cholesterol from these foods. Eating cholesterol is the only healthy way to block cholesterol production in the body. Eating cholesterol is one of the best things you can do for your body."—Diana Schwarzbein, MD

Homemade Almond or Hazelnut Milk

You can buy organic almond milk or you can make your own. Many store bought milks, even though they are organic contain high amounts of sugar (organic cane juice), so read labels carefully. You will not want to buy store bought boxed almond milk again after you have made it yourself. Your smoothies will definitely taste better. Use organic nuts when making nut milk.

To make almond milk, soak 2½ cups almonds or hazelnuts* overnight in lightly salted water to remove phytates and enzyme inhibitors. Drain, rinse, and re-soak the almonds in fresh water at least once during this process.

In a blender place the almonds with 6 cups of filtered water and a pinch of sea salt. You can also add ½ teaspoon vanilla if you like. Puree the nuts until completely liquefied, being careful not to overheat the mixture. Pour the nut liquid into a cheesecloth lined strainer or nut milk bag. Yields 6 cups.

Keep the leftover almond pulp to put in other recipes, like the Orange Almond Cake or Nora's Coconut Bliss Truffles.

To dry the pulp spread on a sheet pan and place in the oven at 150 degrees. Keep checking until it is dry to the touch. Freeze in zip-lock bags.

*Hazelnuts do not have to be soaked prior to making hazelnut milk, as they do not contain enzyme inhibitors.

Coconut Milk Kefir

Kefir is a fermented milk product similar to yogurt but with more liquid. It's fun to make and you can use it in almost any of these breakfast beverages. Once you begin to make kefir it will become a family ritual. You will need a candy thermometer.

> **3 cans (14 ounces each) coconut milk. Do not use "lite"**
> **1–2 tablespoons raw honey**
> **¼ cup of good quality "plain" (not flavored or sweetened) yogurt**

Method:

In a saucepan bring the coconut milk to 125 degrees and then remove from heat. Cover and cool to 110 degrees. You do not want to add the bacterial culture until the mixture has cooled enough or you will kill the culture.

In a bowl combine the ¼ cup of "plain" yogurt, the honey and ½ cup of the cooled coconut milk and mix well. Then add the rest of the cooled coconut milk to this mixture.

Pour the mixture into a glass bowl, a shallow glass baking dish, or a stainless steel pot and cover with plastic wrap. Set the container in your oven with the light (60 watt bulb) turned on so the temperature in the oven remains at 100–110 degrees constantly for about 24–29 hours.

Too high a heat will kill the culture and too low a heat will prevent the activation of the bacterial enzymes. Temperature stability is the key. When the kefir has set, remove from the oven and refrigerate.

Kumodo Dragon's Milk
"for kids of all ages"

Did you know dragons have green milk? You can make this drink and take it to work for a mid-morning pick me up.

> 1 teaspoon or tablespoon super-green food of your choice (amount depends on you)
> 1 cup almond milk, *well chilled*
> 1 tablespoon raw almond butter
> 1 tablespoon sesame/flax mix
> a packet of Stevita (optional)
> ½ teaspoon vanilla

In the blender, blend all the ingredients together. Add a little more almond milk if it is too thick.

Chocolate Chai

Serves 2 generously

This is a very unusual and deliciously spicy beverage. Choose the spices that please you.

1 black tea bag
½ cup boiling water
¼ teaspoon ground nutmeg
⅛ teaspoon ground pepper
¼ teaspoon cinnamon or one cinnamon stick
1 teaspoon *microplaned* **fresh ginger**
1 teaspoon vanilla
1 packet Stevita or to taste
2 cups organic milk or almond milk
2 tablespoons organic unsweetened cocoa powder. Try Dagoba or Holy Kakow from Portland Oregon

In a small saucepan, pour boiling water over the teabag. Let steep for five minutes. Remove bag.

Heat the milk in a saucepan until it reaches the boiling point.

In a bowl combine the cocoa powder, stevia, spices and vanilla. Whisk in the hot milk and then the steeped tea. Re-heat, if necessary, but do not boil. Pour into mugs.

Chocolate Mexicano

Hot chocolate is no longer just a drink for the kids. Authentic Mexican chocolate is made with dark chocolate, vanilla, ground almonds, and a variety of spices such as pepper, cinnamon, nutmeg, and chiles. All these ingredients are added to hot milk and then "frothed" with a hand carved wooden tool called a molino. You can buy a molino at a Mexican food specialty shop.

Mexican Chocolate, *"Caliente"*

Serves 2

> 2 cups almond milk or whole milk
> 4 tablespoons organic unsweetened cocoa powder (Holy Kakao or Dagoba)
> 1 Stevita packet, or drops, to taste
> ½ teaspoon vanilla
> dashes of your choice of spices, cinnamon, nutmeg, chile powder or fresh ground pepper
> Serve with cinnamon sticks

For garnish whip some heavy cream (softly), sweetened with a very little stevia.

Mix the cocoa, spices and stevia together in a small bowl.

Heat the milk to the boiling point a saucepan and whisk in the cocoa, spice mixture. Whisk until frothy. Add the vanilla and pour into two mugs.

Mint Chocolate Smoothie

Serves 2

> 2 cups well chilled almond milk (chill in freezer for ½ hour until slushy)
> 2 teaspoons green *Superfood* of your choice
> 1 heaping tablespoon raw organic cocoa powder
> ½ teaspoon vanilla
> 1 packet Stevita or (to taste)
> 8–10 spearmint leaves

Blend all the ingredients well and pour into frosty glasses. Raw organic cocoa is very high in antioxidants.

Berry Smoothie

Serves 2–3

> 1 cup frozen organic strawberries, blueberries or raspberries
> 2 tablespoons ground sesame/flaxseed mix
> I packet Stevita (optional)
> 2 tablespoons raw almond butter
> 2 cups almond milk

Blend ingredients adding filtered water if necessary to achieve the right consistency.

Cardamom Lassi

Serves 2

This is a classic Indian yogurt drink that's great for breakfast.

> 2 cups plain organic yogurt
> I tablespoon raw honey or 1 packet Stevita
> 1 scant teaspoon ground cardamom

Put ingredients in a blender and blend until combined. Pour into chilled glasses or place in freezer for 30 minutes until very cold.

Strawberry Sunrise

Serves 4

A beautiful way to begin the day.

> 2 cups *frozen* organic strawberries
> 2 cups fresh *red* grapefruit juice, from whole grapefruit
> ⅓ cup coconut milk
> 1 packet Stevita (optional)
> 4 tablespoons ground sesame, flax mix

Place all ingredients in the blender and puree until very smooth.

Pina Colada Breakfast

Serves 2

1 cup fresh or frozen pineapple chunks (freeze the pineapple chunks in 1 cup amounts)
½ can, (6–7 ounces) coconut milk (cans are 13.5 oz)
1 teaspoon vanilla
1 packet Stevita
2 tablespoons ground sesame-flax mix
filtered water (from your Brita)

Place the ingredients in the blender and puree until very smooth. With the blender running add cold water until the mixture is the consistency that you like. For a frappe, use the *frozen* pineapple.

The Breakfast Bar

This is a great way to stay organized for a family on the go. At home we have a tray that sits on the island counter. On the tray are glass jars filled with *organic* seeds and nuts so people can use anything they want on their morning yogurt, in their smoothies or on their salads or dinner entrée. Make it one of the kid's daily jobs to keep the jars filled from the main stock in the pantry. I haven't added raisins, dried cranberries and blueberries to this list because they are really high in sugars. It's better to use fresh or frozen berries. So I leave that choice up to you.

Favorites are:

pumpkin seeds	sunflower seeds	pecans
walnuts	raw cashews	dried coconut flakes
pine nuts	almonds	your favorite *supergreen* food

In the refrigerator keep all the breakfast items on one shelf . . .
Plain organic yogurt, coconut milk yogurt or kefir, heavy cream, berries, eggs, almond milk, leftover veggies, cooked quinoa, raw almond butter and a jar of ½ & ½ ground sesame and flax seeds so it's easy to grab everything and set it out. Once everything is on the counter everyone can choose his or her own favorite breakfast items easily.

Eggs with Caramelized Onions and Cheese

Serves 4

2 tablespoons KerryGold butter
1 small sweet onion, sliced
8 eggs, beaten
2 teaspoons fresh thyme
4 ounces soft goat cheese or New Zealand* *grass-fed* **cheddar or raw domestic jack or cheddar**

In a small frying pan, over medium heat, sauté the onions in the butter until very soft and brown. Remove and set aside. Whisk eggs and thyme in a bowl. Salt & pepper to taste. Add the beaten eggs to the skillet and cook until soft.

Divide the eggs onto three or four plates and top eggs with caramelized onions and crumbled goat cheese. Sprinkle with more fresh thyme.

*You can find the New Zealand grass-fed cheddar at Trader Joe's. It is very reasonably priced.

Poached Eggs with Asparagus and Hollandaise Sauce

Serves 4

Hollandaise adds luxury to this simple breakfast. You can also use wilted spinach as the base for the eggs to replicate Eggs Florentine, *without the English muffin base*. If you have leftover hollandaise, just refrigerate it and use it on your dinner veggies.

> 4 large organic eggs, poached to desired doneness
> 1 bunch asparagus, end trimmed and steamed
> pinch sea salt and twist of pepper

The Hollandaise:
> 1 cube KerryGold or another *grass-fed* butter
> 1 egg yolk
> ½ teaspoon Dijon mustard
> 1–2 tablespoons fresh lemon juice
> pinch sea salt, dash cayenne or white pepper

In a small saucepan heat the butter to the boiling point. In a blender place the egg yolk, Dijon mustard, and lemon juice. With the blender running slowly pour the hot butter until the hollandaise emulsifies to the consistency of "thin" mayonnaise. You may not have to use all the butter. Season to taste with the sea salt and cayenne.

To serve, divide the asparagus onto four plates. Top the asparagus with the poached eggs and a dollop of hollandaise. Serve immediately while hot.

Eggs with Asparagus and Parmesan

For 2

A simple, elegant breakfast!

2 duck eggs or 4 *pastured* **eggs**
10 very fresh, large asparagus spears, tough bottom trimmed
6 tablespoons KerryGold butter
Celtic sea salt and twist of black pepper

Garnish: grated parmesan

In a medium saucepan bring 2 quarts lightly salted water to a boil. Blanch the asparagus for about 2 minutes or less, depending on size of the asparagus. Remove immediately and plunge in cold water.

In a heavy bottomed skillet, heat 3 tablespoons of the butter over high heat and heat the asparagus spears seasoning with a pinch of sea salt and some freshly ground pepper. Remove the spears and fan them out onto two dinner plates.

After wiping out the skillet with a paper towel, add the remaining butter and heat the pan to medium. Crack the two duck eggs in the pan, taking care not to break the yolks. Cook the eggs gently, sunny side up, until the whites are done. Season the eggs with a pinch of salt and some pepper.

Remove the eggs carefully with a wide spatula and place on top of the asparagus. Grate the parmesan liberally on top of the eggs. A very impressive dish!

Baked Eggs in Ramekins

These eggs are wonderfully rich and creamy and will keep you satisfied for hours.

One ramekin per person

> **1—6 ounce ramekin, liberally buttered**
> **2** *pastured or range-fed* **chicken eggs or one duck egg**
> **2 tablespoons whipping cream**
> **Pinch sea salt, twist of pepper**

Garnish: chopped fresh thyme, tarragon, savory or parsley

Preheat oven to 350 degrees. Place the eggs in the buttered ramekin. Place the ramekin in a baking dish and pour boiling water ½ up the outside of the ramekin. Bake the eggs for 15 minutes or until just set. Remove from the oven and sprinkle with the fresh herbs if desired.

Poached Duck Eggs with Spinach and Parmesan Zabaglione

For 4

Fabulously Rich!

1 duck egg per person
4 tablespoons KerryGold butter
One heaping handful of baby spinach per person
Celtic sea salt and a twist of pepper

In a vegetable steamer, over boiling water quickly wilt the spinach. Remove to plates kept in a warm oven.

In a large heavy bottomed skillet melt 4 tablespoons of butter and bring the heat up to medium-high. Crack the eggs into the pan and cook without turning for 4–5 minutes until the white is done. Season with sea salt and pepper. Remove the eggs to the plates of warmed spinach. Top each plate with the egg and then a dollop of the zabaglione. Grate some additional Parmesan on top.

Parmesan Zabaglione
The zabaglione is great on grilled vegetables too.

5 egg yolks
1½ tablespoons freshly ground black pepper
⅔ cup dry Marsala
½ cup organic whipping cream
3 tablespoons Parmesan

To begin set up a bowl of ice water to place the zabaglione over when it is time to cool. Whip the ½ cup of whipping cream and ½ tablespoon of pepper to stiff peaks, then fold in the Parmesan. Place the bowl in the refrigerator while making the zabaglione.

In a large stainless steel bowl whisk the egg yolks with the Marsala and 1 tablespoon of the pepper until foamy. Then place the bowl over a large saucepan of simmering water and continue whisking until the mixture is thick and begins to mound. This will take about 10 minutes. Remove the zabaglione to the bowl with the ice bath and place over the top, continue to whisk until the mixture is cool, then fold in the chilled whipped cream mixture.

Vegetable Hash

Serves 4–6

Whatever vegetables you have left from dinner can be thrown into this easy dish.

> 8 large eggs, beaten
> 2 cups leftover cooked vegetables (the Pesto Vegetables are fabulous)
> twist of pepper, pinch of salt
> 2 tablespoons KerryGold butter
> 2 teaspoons fresh parsley or other fresh herbs

Garnish: grated New Zealand grass-fed cheddar or Parmesan cheese

Heat the butter in a large non-stick skillet. Add the vegetables and heat thoroughly. Pour the beaten eggs (salt & pepper the eggs) into the skillet and stir gently until they begin to set. Keep stirring the eggs until they are just done, but still soft. Add the grated cheese and fresh herbs at the very end if desired.

To serve plate the eggs while hot. Serve with homemade salsa or Tabasco Sauce.

Japanese Scrambled Eggs

Serves 4

This is an unusual and delicious breakfast choice.

Vegetables

    2 tablespoons cold pressed sesame oil

    8 large shitake mushrooms, sliced very thin

    ½ cup red bell pepper, sliced thin

    ½ pound snow peas, sliced thin on the diagonal

    3 ounces pickled ginger, chopped

    6 tablespoons Nama Shoyu or San-J *wheat free* tamari

    1 tablespoon rice wine vinegar

Eggs

    2 tablespoons KerryGold butter or ghee

    6 eggs, beaten

    2 teaspoons Nama Shoyu or San-J Tamari

Garnish: 1 scallion, sliced very thin on the diagonal (optional)

In a large sauté pan heat the sesame oil over medium heat, add the mushrooms and cook until soft. Add the bell pepper, snow peas, pickled ginger, Nama Shoyu and rice wine vinegar. Mix well. Put a lid on the pan and remove from heat.

In a small bowl beat the eggs with the Nama Shoyu. In a small sauté pan heat the butter over medium heat. Scramble the eggs gently until just set.

To serve place equal portions of the vegetables on 4 plates. Top with the eggs and serve hot.

Garnish with the scallions.

Breakfast or Lunch Burrito

Protein *to go!* This is a great, hearty breakfast for teenagers on the move.

> 1 Ezekiel sprouted corn or grain tortilla, or use rice tortillas if
> you are gluten sensitive
> 2 eggs, beaten
> 1 teaspoon KerryGold butter
> pinch sea salt

Garnish: finely chopped onion, cilantro, avocado or grated raw cheese (optional). Salsa!

In a large pan over medium high heat, toast the tortilla on both sides. Remove to a plate. In the same pan add the butter and cook the eggs until desired doneness. Salt and pepper to taste. Remove the tortilla from the oven and add the eggs. Garnish with your choice of ingredients.

Chicken Sausages and Vegetables

Try Bruce Aidells' or Amylu chicken sausages with *no grain fillers.* They are so delicious you won't believe it. Make sure your grocer knows about them.

In a large pan, with 1 tablespoon sesame or coconut oil, sauté one sausage per person until brown. Add some leftover veggies from dinner or add some sliced onion to the pan and then some tomatoes or spinach. Be creative. When the vegetables are heated through serve hot.

Coconut Milk Quinoa

Serves 4

A creamy, *comfort food*, breakfast.

Quinoa's natural *saponin* coating must be removed before it's ready for cooking. The common method is to soak it over night and rinse it the next morning before cooking. You can make enough for several breakfasts and keep it handy in the refrigerator.

> **1 cup organic quinoa**
> **1 can coconut milk, (13.5 ounces)**
> **¼–½ cup water**
> **¼ teaspoon cinnamon or some grated fresh ginger**
> **1 Stevita packet (optional)**
> **pinch sea salt**

Place the quinoa, coconut milk, water, cinnamon and salt in a saucepan. Cover and simmer on low for 15–20 minutes until the quinoa shows little rings. This means that it is done. I usually top mine with ingredients from the breakfast bar, like organic berries, coconut flakes, chopped almonds or pecans, one tablespoon ground sesame and flax seed mix, heavy cream or a dollop of coconut milk. Wow!

Breakfast Ricotta Custard

Serves 6

Comfort food and easy to prepare! Serve with fresh berries! The custard would make an elegant Sunday breakfast or simple evening dessert sprinkled with some of the Nut Crust Mix. The custard tastes like cheesecake.

> **1 pound organic ricotta**
> **1 cup organic sour cream**
> **2 eggs**
> **⅛ cup warmed raw honey or 2–3 packets of stevia to taste**
> **1 teaspoon vanilla**

Garnish: freshly grated nutmeg (use the microplane), chopped nuts, toasted coconut, or berries of your choice. Fresh Raspberry Sauce would also be wonderful.

Preheat the oven to 325 degrees. Liberally butter six 6-ounce ramekins.

In the food processor blend the ingredients until smooth. Pour the mixture into the buttered ramekins. Set the ramekins in a 9 x 13 inch glass pan and pour hot water in the pan to come halfway up the sides. Bake the custards until puffy, about 50 minutes.

To serve, run a sharp knife around the edge of the ramekin and invert onto a dessert plate. If you refrigerate the custards until later, the chilled custards will not be able to invert. But eating them out of the ramekin is just as good.

Breakfast Compote with Yogurt

Serves 2

Dessert for Breakfast? But of course!

1 cup sliced strawberries
¾ cup blueberries
½ cup diced mango
juice of ½ lime
½ cup thick Greek Yogurt with a dash of vanilla

Garnish: Toasted coconut or a sprig of mint

In a bowl place the fruit and then add the lime juice and mix to incorporate.

Using two glass tumblers, or a wide mouth wine glass beginning with the fruit, layer the yogurt and fruit ending with the yogurt.

Sustainable Cuisine
Hors d'oeuvres

When I had my catering company, The Best of Everything, in the Napa Valley, I was well known for my innovative hors d'oeuvres and dips, some of which I marketed in the local grocery stores. I have made all the recipes in this section, *Sustainably Kosher*. For crackers I recommend Lydia's Organics Sunflower Seed Bread or Mary's Gone Crackers. You can purchase the *everydayraw* cookbook by Mathew Kenney and try making your own crackers and chips from the recipes in the book. Making the crackers would be a fun family project.

Party Nut Mix

These nuts are great to keep around the house or to take to work for snacks. To make these nuts follow the directions for soaking and drying the nuts.

> 1¼ cups total (¼ cup each *raw* cashews, almonds, pecans, walnuts and pistachios)
> ¼ cup coconut oil
> ⅛ each teaspoon cumin and cayenne pepper (or more if desired)
> 1 tablespoon raw honey
> Celtic Flower of the Ocean sea salt*

Mix the spices in a cup. Warm the coconut oil, spices and honey over a water bath. Place the nuts in a large bowl. Pour the warm spicy oil mixture over the nuts and mix very well. Place the nut mixture on a stainless sheet pan and roast in the oven at 375 degrees until golden brown. Keep turning the nuts with a spatula while they roast. Remove from oven Sprinkle with the Celtic Flower of the Ocean salt. You can also use Maldon sea salt from England.

*Celtic Flower of the Ocean sea salt is a finishing salt that looks like little snowflakes. It sparkles. You can order it on line at *www.celticseasalt.com*.

Roasted Garlic

This is so simple to do and your family and friends will love you for it. Spread the roasted garlic on Lydia's Organics Sunflower Seed Bread or Mary's Gone Crackers. You can also squeeze the garlic onto cooked vegetables. Use the leftover roasted garlic skins for your homemade vegetable or chicken broth.

> **6 large heads of garlic, with the tips of each section cut off**
> **Brush the heads liberally with extra virgin olive oil**
> **Sprinkle heads with sea salt and a twist of cracked pepper**

Place the heads of garlic in a glass pie pan and cover with foil. Bake the heads at 375 degrees for 1 to 1½ hours until very soft. When done reserve the oil. Drizzle the oil over vegetables or use when you make homemade mayonnaise.

Toasted Goat Cheese

Serves 6

Warm toasted goat cheese is one of the joys of life. Serve the cheese with Lydia's Sunflower Seed Bread or Mary's Gone Crackers. The Toasted Goat Cheese is the perfect accompaniment to a simple green salad.

> ½ cup ground pecans, (macadamia nuts are also fantastic) lightly toasted and ground in the food processor
> 3 tablespoons extra virgin olive oil
> 6 ounces soft goat cheese log, sliced into 6 rounds

Garnish: roasted garlic or oil packed sun dried tomatoes, sliced very thin (optional)

Place the ground pecans on a plate. Pour the olive oil onto another plate. First dip the cheese rounds in the oil and then the ground nuts and place in a glass pie pan. You can refrigerate until you are ready to bake.

In a 400-degree oven, toast the cheese rounds for 3–4 minutes. Watch carefully so the cheese gets soft but does not completely melt. Remove from oven and serve immediately.

Garnish the cheese with the roasted garlic or sun-dried tomatoes.

Bagna Cauda Hot Olive Oil Sauce

Serves 4

The first time I ever tasted this sauce I was about twelve years old. I was invited over to my friend's house for dinner and her mother served it. I couldn't stop eating. The recipe is from Piedmont and translates as "hot bath." Serve with lots of raw or cooked vegetables as a party appetizer, or serve it with your vegetables for dinner. Try it with steamed artichokes for a dipping sauce.

> ½ cup extra virgin olive oil
> 1 cube KerryGold butter
> 6 cloves garlic, minced
> ⅛ teaspoon red chile flakes (optional)
> 4 anchovy filets or 3–4 tablespoons anchovy paste (in tube)

In a small saucepan over low heat, warm the olive oil, butter and garlic. Do not brown the garlic.

Add the smashed anchovies or anchovy paste. Heat thoroughly. Transfer to a heated bowl or fondue pot to stay warm.

Coriander Marinated Olives

This recipe is very unusual. I use it later in the salad section to accompany a spinach salad. Marinate the olives for at least 8 hours so the flavors meld.

> ½ pound cracked, but not pitted Cypriot or cerignola olives
> ¼ cup extra virgin olive oil
> ⅛ cup fresh lemon juice, use Meyer lemons, if possible
> 3–4 cloves of garlic, crushed
> 1 tablespoon whole cracked coriander seeds
> ½ lemon, cut into small wedges
> 1 fresh or dried bay leaf cut into quarters

In a glass bowl combine all the ingredients. Cover and refrigerate for at least 8 hours, stirring occasionally. Olives will keep for a month. Bring olives to room temperature before serving.

Olives with Orange and Fennel

Olives make a healthy snack. These olives are fragrant with fennel and orange.

8 ounces *each* **French Piccoline, Greek Kalamata, Black oil cured
and Spanish Arbequena olives (or your favorite olive selection)
2 medium fennel bulbs cut lengthwise into eighths
4 organic oranges
8 large cloves garlic, peeled and thinly sliced
¼ teaspoon red pepper flakes
½ teaspoon fennel seed, coarsely cracked
Celtic Flower of Ocean salt**

With a vegetable peeler, remove 16 strips of orange peel 2" long. Remove any white pith with the knife. Bring a large pot of water to a boil. Add the fennel slices and cook for three minutes. Drain in a colander in the sink.

In a large saucepan warm the olive oil. Add the orange peel, fennel, fennel seed, garlic and red pepper flakes and cook until the mixture is sizzling, about 1 minute. Add the olives and keep warm for about 5 minutes. Remove from heat and let sit for six hours. Discard the orange peel.

You can make the olives the day before the party. When you serve the olives, sprinkle lightly with the Celtic salt. You can also use the olives as a garnish with a green salad. Olives make a healthy snack.

Magical Muhamara from Syria

I call this recipe the "thinking man's hummus." It's my favorite dip of all. We packaged it and sold it under The Best of Everything label in the Napa and Sonoma area. Serve the dip with Lydia's Sunflower Seed Bread, Mary's Gone Crackers or raw or vegetables. This is an unusual and delicious sauce for grilled fish.

> 1½ cups lightly toasted walnuts (prepare nuts by soaking and rinsing first)
> 4 large roasted, skinned and seeded red bell peppers (you can use roasted peppers in a jar)
> 2 teaspoons ground cumin
> 4 large cloves garlic, minced
> 4 tablespoons pomegranate molasses (Middle Eastern specialty store or chefshop.com)
> juice of ½ lemon
> 1 tablespoon red chili pepper flakes
> ¼ cup (or more) extra virgin olive oil
> sea salt to taste and a twist of black pepper

Toast the walnuts on a sheet pan at 350 degrees for about 10 minutes, turning a few times to toast evenly.

Combine all the ingredients in the food processor and puree until very smooth. Adjust the seasonings to suite your taste. You may want more lemon, cumin, or garlic. Muhamara will keep in the refrigerator in a jar topped with olive oil for about 2 weeks. You can also freeze it.

When serving drizzle a little olive oil and sprinkle some ground cumin on top for garnish.

Endive "Spoons" with Lemon-Herb Goat Cheese

These appetizers are simple to make but impressive to serve at a party.

1 pound soft goat cheese
2 tablespoons lemon juice
2 teaspoons lemon zest
2 tablespoons extra virgin olive oil
3 tablespoons fresh chives, finely chopped
8 heads Belgian endive, red or white
6 organic cherry tomatoes, sliced very thin crosswise

Garnish: cilantro or Italian flat leaf parsley (leaves only)

Blend goat cheese, lemon juice, zest, and olive oil in the food processor. Stir in the chives. This can be done the day ahead and refrigerate.

Before serving separate the endive leaves and arrange on a platter, Spoon small amounts of the cheese mixture on the "spoon" end of the endive. Garnish with a thin slice of the tomato and a cilantro leaf.

Pacific Rim Tuna "Salsa"

Serves 8

This Asian tuna recipe will wake up your taste buds. It has sensational flavor so make plenty. Serve with on cucumber rounds, small *gluten-free* rice crackers or the Lydia's Sunflower Seed Bread. The Tuna Salsa may also be served on a butter lettuce or radicchio leaf as a first course.

16 ounces *sashimi grade* **tuna (figure two ounces per person if serving as an hors d'oeuvres)**
1 ripe avocado, finely diced
Juice of 4–5 limes
1–2 jalapeno chilies, seeded and finely diced
3 tablespoons sesame oil
4 tablespoons coconut milk
2 tablespoons sesame seeds
Nama Shoyu soy sauce or San-J *wheat-free* **organic tamari, to taste**
1 tablespoon grated fresh ginger, or to taste
8 heads red or white Belgian endive

Finely dice the tuna and place in a bowl. Add the remaining ingredients. Stir very gently so as not to mash the avocado. You will want to see the avocado pieces clearly. Spoon this very tasty mixture onto the separated leaves of the endive. Sprinkle with additional sesame seeds if desired. Serve immediately.

Salmon Rillettes

Makes 4 cups

Rillettes are a very rich and unusual French appetizer to serve with some tasty crackers or rounds of English cucumber. It's best to prepare the rillettes the day before serving to let the flavors develop.

1 can Alaskan Sockeye Salmon, 14 ounces
8 tablespoons KerryGold butter or another grass-fed butter
½ cup organic whipping cream
2 tablespoons dry white vermouth
2 tablespoons fresh lemon juice
½ pound thinly sliced smoked salmon, cut into pieces
2 tablespoons salt cured capers, rinsed
1 bunch scallions, minced
½ cup fresh dill
pinch of cayenne and a twist of pepper

In the food processor, puree the canned salmon, cream, vermouth, and lemon juice until smooth. Add the smoked salmon, capers, scallions, dill, cayenne and pepper and pulse the ingredients until just mixed, but not blended. Taste for pepper balance. Pack the rillettes in an attractive crock or bowl, cover and refrigerate.

To serve let the rillettes come to room temperature. Place the crock on a large platter and surround with the crackers and cucumber rounds.

Smoked Salmon with Spicy Mango Salsa

Serves 8

This is a tastier version of the familiar smoked salmon and cream cheese. Serve with Lydia's Sunflower Seed bread or rounds of English cucumber. This appetizer would be good served for lunch with a salad of arugula or mesclun.

> **8 ounces of pre-sliced smoked salmon**
> **8 ounces of organic cream cheese, softened**

Salsa:
> **Flesh from two mangoes, finely diced**
> **2 scallions, white & light green part, minced**
> **½ cup fresh cilantro, chopped**
> **3 tablespoons fresh lime juice (one large lime)**
> **1 packet Stevita or to taste (optional)**
> **2 tablespoons Nama Shoyu or San-J** *wheat-free* **tamari**
> **1 teaspoon Asian chile sauce**

Garnish: additional cilantro leaves

In a bowl mix all the ingredients for the salsa and refrigerate until ready for use. In another small bowl beat the cream cheese until light and fluffy.

    To serve spread some cream cheese on the sunflower bread triangles or a round of cucumber. Lay a small piece of smoked salmon on top. Garnish with a cilantro leaf.

Thai Beef Satay

Makes approximately 20 satay

These delicious appetizers are served with the Spicy Peanut Sauce. They are a big hit at any party. You can serve them for dinner too. When making this recipe the beef has to marinate at least 2 hours or overnight.

> **1½ pounds of** *grass-fed* **beef flank steak***

Marinade:
> 1¾ cups coconut milk
> 1 teaspoon Nama Shoyu soy sauce or San-J *wheat-free* tamari
> 1 teaspoon yellow curry powder
> 1 teaspoon ground turmeric
> 1 teaspoon *microplaned* ginger
> 20 bamboo skewers soaked in water for an hour

Garlic Coconut Milk:
> ½ teaspoon cold pressed sesame oil
> ½ teaspoon minced garlic
> ¾ coconut milk

In a bowl combine the coconut milk, tamari, spices and grated ginger. Set aside.

Cut the flank steak across the grain, holding the knife at an angle to the cutting surface so that each slice is about 1½ inches wide and ⅛ inch thick. There should be about 20 strips.

Thread each strip of beef lengthwise on a skewer. You may want to wrap the ends of the skewers in foil so they won't burn.

Start your fire and bring the coals to medium-high heat. Adjust the grill to about 4 inches above the coals.

Place the skewers on the grill, as many as will fit. Baste the meat with the Garlic Coconut Milk. Cook for one minute, until grill marks show and then turn and baste the other side. Cook for another minute. Serve immediately with the peanut sauce.

*Chicken breast may also be used. Slice the breast across the grain, as the above directions describe.

Smoked Trout Pate

Serves 4 as an appetizer

Serve this easy pate with crackers, on English cucumber slices, or Belgium endive leaves.

> 4 ounces smoked trout
> ¼ cup organic cream cheese
> 2 tablespoons extra virgin olive oil
> juice of ½ lemon, about 2 tablespoons
> 1 tablespoon creamed horseradish
> ¼ teaspoon cayenne pepper

Place all the ingredients in the food processor and whirl till smooth. This takes a minute. Transfer the mixture to a covered container and refrigerate until ready to serve.

Thai Peanut Sauce

Yields approximately 4 cups

We used to go to the Thai restaurant in Berkeley, Siam Cuisine. All their dishes were first rate. We ordered the grilled chile salad to see who could eat it without crying. It was always a tear jerker. The Siam had the best Peanut Curry Sauce I've ever tasted and this version approximates the original. The peanut sauce is also a great dip for raw vegetables.

1 jar (¼ cup) Thai Red Curry paste
2 tablespoons Mongolian Fire Oil
1 tablespoon ground cayenne pepper
1 tablespoon paprika (for color)
¾ teaspoon cinnamon
½ teaspoon ground cumin
⅛ teaspoon ground cloves
1 tablespoon raw honey or 1 packet Stevita
5¼ cups coconut milk
¼ cup Nama Shoyu soy sauce or San-J tamari
⅔ cup organic vegetable broth
2 tablespoons creamy organic peanut butter or almond butter
(if you cannot eat peanuts)

Combine the curry paste, Mongolian Fire Oil, cayenne, paprika, cinnamon, cumin, cloves, honey or Stevita, Nama Shoyu and 1¾ cups of the coconut milk in a large saucepan. Bring the ingredients to a boil over medium heat and cook, stirring occasionally for 5 minutes until all the ingredients are well blended.

Add the vegetable broth and the remaining 3½ cups of coconut milk one cup at a time, whisking with each addition and keeping the sauce boiling gently. Then, reduce the sauce and cook for 25–30 minutes until the oil starts to appear on the top of the sauce. Make sure the sauce does not burn on the bottom. Add more vegetable broth or a little water if necessary. Just before removing from the heat, add the peanut butter and whisk until blended. To serve, pour the warm sauce onto a plate and dip your grilled chicken or seafood satay (skewers) in the sauce.

Goat Cheese and Basil Dip

Makes 2 cups

This is a wonderful dip for party vegetables but it would also be great on some steamed asparagus or broccolini.

½ cup homemade mayonnaise
1 cup fresh goat cheese, softened to room temp.
1 cup *very fresh* basil leaves
½ cup organic whipping cream
juice of ½ lemon
Celtic sea salt and a twist of pepper

Place all ingredients in the food processor and blend till smooth.

Scallop Ceviche with Avocado-Mango Salsa and Belgium Endive

Serves 8

I ate a lot of ceviche in Mexico. The Mexicans would eat it for breakfast at a little stand in La Penita de Jaltemba where I had my house. They even served a warm ceviche, which was quite unusual. This is a very colorful rendition, which I know you will enjoy. As a first course serve 3 ounces of the ceviche in a butter lettuce or radicchio cup.

> 16 ounces scallops, coarsely chopped
> 4 avocados, finely diced
> 1 red bell pepper, seeded and finely diced
> 2 ripe mangoes, peeled, pit removed and finely diced
> juice of 2 limes

Fusion Dressing:
> ¼ cup fresh cilantro leaves chopped
> 1 scallion, finely minced
> 1 clove garlic, finely minced
> 3 tablespoons fresh lime juice (one large lime)
> 3 tablespoons fresh orange juice
> 4 tablespoons extra virgin olive oil
> 1 packet Stevita or drops, to taste (optional)
> 1 teaspoon Asian chile sauce
> 1 tablespoon *microplaned* ginger
> pinch sea salt
> 3–4 heads of red or white Belgian endive leaves

Garnish: additional cilantro leaves

Combine scallops, avocadoes, red pepper, and mango in a bowl. Squeeze lime juice over the ingredients and mix gently.

In a bowl whisk together the dressing ingredients. Toss the scallop mixture in the dressing and mix carefully so avocado and mango do not get mushy. You can now keep the ceviche in the refrigerator until time to serve.

Put a small amount of the ceviche on each Belgian endive leaf and arrange them on a colorful platter. Garnish with a cilantro leaf.

Satisfying Soups

Homemade Vegetable or Chicken Broth

Homemade broth is fun to make. This broth is so good you can eat it as a soup. If you have leftover chicken bones from roasting a chicken, add them to the pot. Make a big batch and freeze it so you have it on hand. The chicken fat from homemade stock is rich and nourishing for the body. The gelatin from the bones is an anti-inflammatory. No wonder chicken soup is good for us when we are sick.

¼ cup cold pressed sesame oil
8 cups sliced onions
4 cups diced carrots
2 cups chopped celery, including tops
4 cups sliced leeks, all parts (rinsed of dirt)
3 cups diced parsnips
leftover cobs from corn, if you have them
2 bulbs of garlic, cut in half
5 cups organic plum tomatoes, plus the juice
6 quarts water
2 cups dry white wine
6 Bay leaves
2 teaspoons whole black peppercorns
few sprigs of fresh thyme
2 cups roughly chopped parsley, washed well

In a very large pot brown the vegetables in the oil. Add the plum to-matoes, seasonings & herbs, water and white wine. You can use leftover baked garlic bulbs, too, if you like. Bring the ingredients to a boil and then reduce heat and simmer for 2 to 2½ hours. Remove from heat and cool. Strain the stock through a fine sieve. Chill the stock and skim off any fat. Pour the stock into glass jars and use within a week or freeze.

Late Summer Melon Soup with Coconut Milk

Serves 4

An unusual soup you can make ahead. Very richly scented with the basil and mint.

3 pounds very ripe and fragrant summer melon
1 can coconut milk
juice of 2 limes
zest of one lime
2 teaspoons *microplaned* ginger
1–2 jalapenos seeded and finely diced
1 tablespoon garden basil leaves, chopped (Thai basil if you have it)
1 tablespoon chopped mint
pinch of sea salt, to taste

Garnish: toasted unsweetened coconut (optional) sprigs of mint

Peel and seed the melon and cut the flesh into chunks, reserving ½ cup of finely diced melon.

In the food processor puree the melon. While the machine is running pour in the coconut milk, herbs, jalapeno, (add one and taste) lime juice and zest. Chill the soup for several hours before serving.

To serve pour into wide mouth red wine glasses and garnish with the toasted coconut and a sprig of mint.

Summer Squash Soup with Mint Pesto

Serves 8

Did you ever wonder what to do with all those summer squash in the garden? Well, this recipe with the tasty mint pesto is the answer.

The Soup:
> 1 stick KerryGold butter
> 1 medium sweet onion, sliced thin
> 2 pounds yellow or green summer squash, halved and thinly sliced
> 2 carrots, thinly sliced
> 4 cups homemade chicken stock
> ½ teaspoon Celtic sea salt
> ¼ cup organic whipping cream (optional for extra richness)

The Pesto:
> 1 cup fresh mint leaves
> ⅔ cup Italian flat leaf parsley leaves
> 2 scallions, chopped
> 1 clove garlic
> 4 tablespoons pine nuts
> ¼ cup extra virgin olive oil (more if needed)
> 1 teaspoon lemon juice
> pinch sea salt, twist of black pepper

In a large heavy bottomed soup pot melt the butter over medium heat. Cook the onion until softened, season with the salt. Add the squash, carrot and stock and bring to a simmer. Partially cover the pot and cook until the vegetables are tender, about 20 minutes. Remove from heat and let cool about 15–20 minutes.

When the soup is cool enough, puree in small batches in the blender until very smooth. Return the soup to the soup pot (having wiped it out) and re-heat the soup, adding the whipping cream just before serving.

While the soup is simmering pulse the mint and parsley leaves, scallions, garlic and the pine nuts until finely chopped. Add the lemon juice, salt and pepper. While the processor is running, slowly add the olive oil until the mixture forms a paste. Thin the mixture with a little water if necessary to achieve the right consistency.

To serve, ladle the soup into bowls and swirl a tablespoon of the pesto into the soup. If you have leftover pesto, place it in a glass jar and cap with a little olive oil. Use the pesto within 3 days, perhaps on some vegetables for dinner.

Avgolemono, Greek Egg and Lemon Soup

Serves 8

I used to make this lovely soup at Pauli's Café in San Francisco. The recipe works best with homemade chicken stock because it needs the richness of the chicken fat. This variation is made with quinoa, which makes it a higher protein soup.

> 8–10 cups homemade chicken stock
> 2 cups quinoa, soaked overnight and rinsed
> 4 tablespoons KerryGold butter
> 1 teaspoon Celtic sea salt and a twist of pepper
> 2 tablespoons organic, non-GMO corn starch (Rapunzel or Rumford)
> 4 large eggs
> ¾ cup fresh lemon juice

Garnish: three slices of avocado per bowl of soup and a very thin slice of lemon

In a large saucepan over medium heat bring 6 cups of the stock and the butter to a boil. Add the quinoa and cook until done, about 15 minutes. Season with the sea salt and pepper. Remove from heat and let cool for 15 minutes.

Dissolve corn starch in ½ cup water. Heat the remaining stock until just hot, but not boiling.

In the blender place the eggs, cornstarch and lemon juice. With the blender running slowly add the remaining 2 cups of stock and blend until the mixture begins to thicken. Pour the mixture into another soup pot. Now blend the soup mixture with the quinoa in batches and add it to the egg mixture.

Reheat the soup while whisking to simmer, but do not boil. Remove from heat and ladle into the soup bowls and garnish with the avocado slices and lemon.

*For a higher protein variation add 2–3 ounces of leftover cooked chicken to each bowl of soup.

Thai Green Curry Chowder

Serves 10

I think I like Thai green curry better than red curry. This soup is rich and complex and not too hot. You may substitute other vegetables in place of the bok choy if you prefer. If this recipe seems like too much you can make the soup base and freeze some. Thaw when needed for another meal.

Soup Base:
    8 ounces KerryGold butter
    1 cup diced yellow onion
    1 red or green Thai chile or jalapeno, seeded and minced
    ¼ cup chopped garlic
    1 can coconut milk
    2 cups dry white wine
    4 cups organic vegetable broth, preferably homemade
    4 tablespoons organic tomato paste
    4 tablespoons green curry paste (more or less)
    juice of 1 lime (or more to taste)

Soup Ingredients:
    ¼ cup coconut oil
    12 baby bok choy, trimmed of tough outer leaves
    1 cup corn kernels
    8 ounces enoki mushrooms (optional)
    ¼ cup petite peas, fresh or frozen
    8 ounces uncooked medium shrimp, peeled and de-veined, tails removed
    8 ounces bay scallops
    3 tablespoons chopped mint

Garnish: cilantro sprigs and thin lime slices

In a large soup pot over medium heat, melt the butter. Add the onion, minced chile, and garlic and sauté until they are soft. Add the wine, coconut milk, tomato paste, curry paste and stock; reduce the heat to low and simmer for 35–40 minutes. Add the lime juice.

In a separate pan over medium heat, warm the coconut oil. Add the bok choy and sauté until it is still a bit crisp, not too soft (about 10 minutes). Add the shrimp and scallops and cook for 3–4 minutes, stirring to mix well.

Add the seafood/bok choy mixture to the soup base. Just before removing the soup from the heat, stir in the chopped mint, corn and peas. Ladle into bowls and garnish with the cilantro sprigs and lime slices. Serve hot.

Hearty Vegetable Soup with Pesto

Serves 10

This soup is dinner in a bowl. The homemade pesto is what makes this soup so special.

> 2 tablespoons cold pressed sesame oil
> 1 large onion, diced
> ½ cup diced red bell pepper
> 2 large carrots, diced
> 1 leek, white and light part only, washed and diced
> 3 tablespoons garlic, minced
> ½ head green cabbage, thinly sliced
> ½ cup broccoli or cauliflower, cut into small pieces
> 1 bouquet garni (herb bundle) of 6 sprigs of flat leaf parsley, six sprigs of thyme, and two bay leaves, tied with a string
> 6–8 cups vegetable broth or chicken stock
> sea salt & ground pepper to taste
> Grated Parmesan cheese, for passing

In a large soup pot over medium heat, warm the oil. Add the onion, bell pepper, carrots, leek and garlic. Saute until the vegetables are tender.

Add the cabbage, broccoli, and the bouquet garni. Slowly add the vegetable broth while heating the soup until the soup is thick with the vegetables, not watery. Season to taste with the salt and pepper.

Pour the soup into bowls and top each with a spoonful of Homemade Pesto. Serve hot, passing the grated Parmesan cheese.

The Pesto:

- 6–8 large cloves garlic
- 2 large bunches basil leaves (about 4 cups)
- ½ cup pine nuts
- juice of ½ lemon
- ⅔ cup grated Parmesan Cheese
- 1 cup extra virgin olive oil
- 1 teaspoon sea salt & twist of pepper to taste

In a food processor, combine the garlic, basil, oregano, pine nuts, lemon juice, and the Parmesan. Turn on the processor and slowly pour in the olive oil; whirl until the mixture is very smooth, adding more oil if necessary. Season with the salt and pepper. Use the pesto immediately.

*Pack the leftover pesto, if there is any, in small jars topped with olive oil and refrigerate for up to a week, or just freeze.

Winter Root Vegetable Soup with Dried Mushrooms

Serves 4

This silky soup is pure luxury. For a very elegant dinner, instead of using the dried porcini mushrooms, shave 1½ ounces fresh black truffle over the soup, or drizzle the soup with truffle oil.

1½ ounces dried porcini, or chanterelle mushrooms
2 tablespoons unsalted butter
¼ cup washed & sliced leek, white part only
1 parsnip, peeled, cored and chopped
¾ cup peeled and chopped celery root
1 sprig of fresh thyme
¼ cup red skin potato, peeled & diced
¼ teaspoon sea salt, plus more for seasoning
1 cup water
¾ cup vegetable broth
½ cup heavy cream
dash white pepper

Cover the mushrooms with warm water and let soak until re-hydrated. Drain well and set aside.

In a large saucepan over medium heat, warm the butter. Stir in the leek, parsnip, potato, celeryroot, thyme and the ¼ teaspoon salt; cook until the leak is translucent. Add the cup of water and simmer, covered, until almost all the water has evaporated (about 10 minutes). Stir in the broth and simmer, covered, for another 15 minutes.

Transfer the mixture to a blender and whirl until it is very smooth, and then transfer it back into the saucepan. For a smoother, more refined soup, strain the mixture through a fine sieve back into the saucepan.

In the same blender, whirl the re-hydrated mushrooms into a paste. Add the mushroom paste and the heavy cream to the soup. Season the soup with sea salt. Reheat the soup slowly before serving. If you are using the truffles, shave them on top of the soup after ladling the soup into the bowls.

Bay Scallop and Root Vegetable Chowder with Leeks

Serves 6

If you like clam chowder, you will love this soup. It makes the perfect first course for Christmas dinner or a simple Sunday supper entrée with a salad.

¼ pound each turnips, carrots and parsnips
peeled and cut into small square pieces (fine dice)
1 pound bay scallops*
2 tablespoons KerryGold butter
3 leeks, white & light green part, washed and thinly sliced
2 jalapenos, seeded and minced
2 medium red bell pepper, finely diced
3 cups homemade vegetable broth
2 bottles clam juice
¾ cup whipping cream
¼ cup minced Italian parsley
1 teaspoon fresh thyme leaves
sea salt & freshly ground pepper

Cover the vegetables with lightly salted water and cook until soft, then drain. In a saucepan melt the butter and cook the leeks, jalapeno and the red bell pepper over medium heat, covered, for about 10 minutes.

Add the broth and the clam juice to the leek mixture, then the cooked vegetable mixture and thyme. Just before serving add the scallops and the cream to the hot soup. It is important not to overcook the scallops. They should just poach briefly in the hot broth. Remove the soup from the heat and season with salt & pepper to taste.

*bay scallops are farmed, and some come from China. See the Blue Ocean Institute Web site *www.blueocean.org/programs.seafood-search*

Curried Onion and Ginger Soup

Serves 6

Caramelized onions, ginger and curry mingle together in this unusual soup.

> 2 tablespoons coconut oil
> 2 pounds Walla Walla, Vidalia or other sweet onion
> ½ cup finely chopped ginger, skin removed
> 1 small jalapeno seeded and chopped
> 1½ teaspoons Madras curry powder
> 1 cup dry white wine
> 1 can coconut milk
> 4 cups homemade chicken stock or vegetable broth
> 1 cup ½ & ½
> 2 tablespoons lime juice
> ½ teaspoon *microplaned* lime zest
> Celtic sea salt and a twist of pepper

Garnish: Sprigs of cilantro

In a large saucepan melt the coconut oil. Add the onions, curry powder, ginger and jalapeno and cook until the onions are caramelized. Add the wine, chicken stock and coconut milk and simmer for another 15 minutes. Remove from the heat and let cool about 10 minutes.

In a blender puree the soup in batches until very smooth. Return the soup to the saucepan and reheat, adding the half & half, lime juice and lime zest. Season the soup again if necessary. This soup can be served hot or prepared ahead and chilled.

Brazilian Shrimp Soup

Serves 6 as a main course

This soup is rich, complex and very festive. If you cannot eat shell-fish, substitute your favorite seasonal vegetables or organic chicken. I recommend corn, red bell peppers and rainbow chard. Serve the soup with a refreshing salad of mesclun, orange sections and the Citrus Vinaigrette.

2 tablespoons coconut oil
1 large onion diced
5 cloves garlic, minced
2 small jalapeno chiles, seeded and finely diced
2 tablespoons *microplaned* ginger
1 pound medium shrimp *with shells* (Northern Canadian Shrimp or Pink Shrimp)* (reserve the shells)
4 cups vegetable broth
8 organic canned plum tomatoes
1 can (13.5 ounces) organic coconut milk
⅔ cup peanut butter
¼ cup fresh lime juice
sea salt & twist of black pepper
¼ cup chopped cilantro
Finely ground peanuts for garnish
Lime wedges for garnish

Remove shells from shrimp and set aside.

In a medium saucepan over medium heat, melt the coconut oil. Add the onion, garlic, chiles, ginger, and the shrimp *shells* (shells only here, not the bodies). Cook over low heat until the onion is translucent. Add the vegetable broth and simmer for 15 minutes.

Strain the broth and return it to the saucepan. Chop the plum to-matoes and add them to the broth. Simmer for 10 minutes.

In a food processor, puree the coconut milk and peanut butter until smooth. Add to the broth. Then add the shrimp bodies and the lime juice. Cook until the shrimp have just turned pink (about 3 min-utes). Add salt and pepper to taste.

Garnish the soup with the chopped cilantro and finely ground peanuts. Serve with the lime wedges.

*avoid farmed shrimp. Check the Blue Ocean Institute Web site *www. blueocean.org/programs,seafood-search*

Chilled "Grilled" Corn and Pepper Soup

Serves 4–6

This is a great chilled summer soup, which can be prepared in advance. It's a great way to use leftover grilled corn from a barbecue. You can also broil the vegetables in your oven.

Vegetables for grilling:
>   2 ears farmer's market, organic corn
>   2 green onions, white and pale parts only
>   ½ pound red bell peppers, stemmed, seeded and halved lengthwise
>   1 jalapeno chile, rinsed, stemmed, seeded and halved lengthwise

Soup Base:
>   4 cups vegetable broth or homemade chicken broth
>   ⅛ cup organic sour cream or crème fraiche
>   1 tablespoon lime juice
>   2 tablespoons chopped cilantro
>   1 teaspoon ground cumin, toasted

Garnish: 1 avocado, lime cream and cilantro sprigs, sea salt and freshly ground pepper

Rub corn, pepper, green onion and jalapeno with sesame oil. Grill the vegetables. Cool and then remove corn from the cob.

If you are using the oven method, brush the corn with oil and broil the ears, turning them often so they brown evenly. To roast the other vegetables, place them in a roasting pan and oil them slightly. Roast in a 400-degree oven, turning often, to roast evenly.

In a blender whirl ½ of the stock with ½ of the vegetables and the sour cream. Blend until smooth. Add the remaining stock, vegetables, cilantro, lime, cumin, salt & pepper to the soup and *chill*. Serve the soup garnished with lime cream, slices of avocado and sprigs of cilantro.

You can also serve this soup hot.

Santa Fe Chipotle Chile Soup

Serves 6

When I lived in Santa Fe I learned about the rich smoky flavor of the Chimayo chile. Serve the soup with the Caesar Salad; a perfect compliment.

2 yellow onions, finely diced
2 carrots, finely diced
2 stalks celery, finely diced
4 cups organic chicken stock
2 tablespoons chipotle chiles (small cans in Mexican section)
1 teaspoon ground cumin
½ teaspoon ground coriander
½ teaspoon dried oregano
4 tablespoons cold pressed sesame oil
1 cup roasted chicken, shredded or additional cooked vegetables of your choice
juice of 2 limes
sea salt and ground pepper

Garnishes:

1¼ cups grated grass-fed New Zealand Cheddar or raw jack cheese
lime cream: 1 cup of sour cream mixed with juice of one lime
avocado slices
lime slices
sprigs of cilantro

In the blender puree the chipotle chiles with 2 tablespoons water. Set aside.

In a large soup pot over medium heat sauté the onion, carrot and celery in the oil until tender. Add one cup of the broth. Cook, covered, until the liquid evaporates and the onions are soft and caramelized. Add the chile puree, remaining broth, cumin, coriander, and oregano. Simmer for 5–10 minutes.

Just before serving, add the chicken or veggies, lime juice, and salt and pepper. Ladle the soup into large soup bowls and garnish with the grated cheese, lime cream, avocado slices and lime slices. Top with sprigs of cilantro.

Spicy Heirloom Tomato Soup

Serves 4

This soup makes a beautiful and zesty first course for a summer lunch or dinner.

> 1 pound ripe heirloom tomatoes or large mixed tomatoes
> 1 medium sweet onion, chopped
> 2 cloves garlic chopped
> 3–4 yellow or orange bell peppers, seeded and chopped, white pith removed
> 2 tablespoons cold pressed sesame oil
> 1 bay leaf
> 1 tablespoon thyme fresh leaves
> 1 teaspoon Chimayo chile powder or Spanish paprika
> 1 tablespoon organic tomato paste
> ¼ cup water
> 1 teaspoon Celtic sea salt & freshly ground pepper
> 1 quart vegetable broth or chicken stock, preferably home-made

Garnish: drizzle of extra virgin olive oil, chopped basil and Italian parsley leaves and slices of avocado (optional)

Cut x's at the base of each tomato and drop them into a pot of boiling water, for 2 minutes. Remove with tongs and set on a plate. When cool, cut in half and squeeze out the seeds, then remove the peeling and dice the remaining tomato.

In a large soup pot heat the oil over medium-high; add the onions, peppers, bay leaf thyme and chile powder. Cook until the onion is soft, stirring a little, and then add the garlic, tomato paste, 1 teaspoon of sea salt, a twist of pepper and the ¼ cup of water. Cook for 5 minutes and then add the tomatoes and the vegetable broth. Cover the soup and simmer for 25 minutes.

To serve, ladle into bowls and garnish with the drizzle of olive oil and the herbs. Top with the slices of avocado for extra richness.

Roasted Garlic Almond Soup

Serves 6

This rich and fragrant roasted garlic soup is fantastic in taste and high in nutrition. It's sure to be a family favorite.

4 heads roasted garlic
4 tablespoons extra virgin olive oil
sea salt and freshly ground black pepper
4 tablespoons KerryGold butter
2 large onions, chopped
½ cup organic whipping cream
10 cups homemade chicken broth (homemade broth is essential)
1 cup dry white wine
1 bay leaf
1 cup toasted almonds, slivered
1 cup *cooked* quinoa

Garnish: chopped Italian parsley leaves, drizzle of olive oil

Preheat the oven to 350 degrees.

Slice the heads of garlic in half and place them in a glass pie plate, cut side up. Spoon the olive oil over the garlic cloves. Sprinkle with a little sea salt and a twist of pepper. Now turn the garlic cut side down and bake for about 30 minutes until very soft and slightly browned. Remove from oven and cool. When the garlic is cool enough squeeze it out from its skin into the food processor. Save the skins for making chicken stock.

In a large stockpot heat the butter to medium. Add the onions and sauté, stirring frequently, until soft and caramelized. Place the cooked onions, and cream in the food processor with the roasted garlic and puree until smooth. Transfer the mixture to a bowl. Wash and dry the food processor bowl.

Using the same stockpot as before, (washed and wiped dry) combine the chicken stock, wine and bay leaf. Bring to a gentle simmer.

Place the toasted almonds and the cooked quinoa in the food processor and process until well blended. Ladle 1 cup of the hot chicken stock into the mixture and process until very smooth.

Whisk the almond-quinoa mixture into the hot stock, then whisk in the garlic-onion puree. Continue whisking until well blended. Correct the seasoning with sea salt and freshly ground pepper to taste.

To serve, ladle the soup into large bowls. Garnish with a drizzle of olive oil and the chopped parsley.

Carrot-Miso Soup

Serves 6

This is a light, delightful soup and the wasabi pea garnish makes a fun taste sensation. The kids will like it.

2 tablespoons cold pressed sesame oil
1 medium leek, (white and light green part) thinly sliced, then rinsed
1 stalk celery chopped
1 teaspoon minced garlic
1½ pounds organic carrots, washed and sliced
1 tablespoon rice wine vinegar
2 tablespoons white miso (or more, to taste)
5 cups vegetable broth
1 packet Stevita (optional)

Garnish: ⅓ cup crushed dried wasabi peas

In a large saucepan over medium heat sauté the leek and the celery in the oil until soft. Add the garlic and cook for 1 minute, add the rice wine vinegar to deglaze the pan and cook for 1 more minute.

Add the carrots, 5 cups of light vegetable broth or water and the miso. Reduce heat to medium-low and cook 30 minutes or until the carrots are tender. Remove soup from the heat and blend (with the Stevita) until very smooth. Reheat the soup if necessary. Taste for seasoning balance and add seas salt if desired.

Serve the soup in bowls and sprinkle some of the wasabi peas on top.

Salad Days

All great salads have *fresh, homemade* salad dressings. I encourage you to use your favorite homemade dressings made with good oils, premium vinegars, freshly squeezed lemon juice, sea salt, and freshly ground pepper. If your kids are old enough have them make their own dressings. It will give everyone a chance to have the fun and responsibility of family food preparation.

Family Style Salad

If you don't want to think of a special salad to make for dinner, just put out the organic lettuce mix and then have small bowls with grated carrots or yellow beets, sprouts, diced avocadoes, red bell pepper and mushroom slices. Let everyone concoct their own salad and add nuts and seeds from the tray. Set the favorite dressings on the table.

Homemade Mayonnaise

Makes 3 cups

Since some of the dressing recipes call for mayonnaise it is essential that you make your own mayo at home out of good oils.

> **2 eggs at room temperature**
> **1 teaspoon Dijon mustard**
> **3 tablespoons lemon juice**
> **1½–2 cups extra virgin olive oil or cold pressed sesame oil (you can mix the two)**
> **pinch of sea salt**

In the blender place the whole eggs, Dijon mustard, lemon juice, and pinch of sea salt. With the blender running, add the oils very slowly until the mixture emulsifies to the desired consistency. Check seasoning for balance. You may want to add more salt, mustard or lemon juice to your taste. Homemade mayonnaise will keep for two weeks.

Red Bell Pepper Mayonnaise

Makes about ¾ cup

The red peppers add pizzazz to the mayonnaise and you can use it in a variety of ways.

> 2 whole roasted red bell peppers, peeled and seeded. Use store bought if you prefer.
> 1 cup Homemade Mayonnaise
> ½ teaspoon red pepper flakes (optional)
> sea salt and pepper

Puree the bell pepper with the mayonnaise in the blender or food processor. Season to taste.

Blue Cheese Dressing

Spoon this dressing on a grilled turkey burger with lettuce and a garden tomato.

> 2 tablespoons extra virgin olive oil
> ¼ small red onion, very thinly sliced
> 1 tablespoon balsamic vinegar
> ¼ teaspoon sea salt
> 3 ounces Maytag or Pt. Reyes Blue cheese
> ¼ cup whipping cream
> Twist of black pepper

In a bowl whisk together the olive oil, onion, vinegar, and salt. In the food processor blend the blue cheese with the cream and then whisk the mixture into the other ingredients. Refrigerate until ready to use.

Citrus Vinaigrette

Citrus vinaigrette is a refreshing choice to use when fruit is in the salad. Great with seafood!

> ¼ cup whole grain mustard
> 1 cup fresh orange juice
> ¼ cup fresh lemon juice
> ¼ cup fresh lime juice
> ⅓ cup Champagne vinegar
> 1 packet Stevita
> 2 tablespoons, each, chopped chervil and chives

1 teaspoon each of organic lemon, & lime zest
1 cup extra virgin olive oil
sea salt & fresh pepper

In a bowl, combine all ingredients & then whisk in the oil. Season to taste with salt and pepper.

Lemon-Oregano Dressing

This dressing is excellent on grilled or roasted vegetables or on a shrimp salad.

¼ cup fresh lemon juice
4 tablespoons balsamic vinegar
¼ cup *fresh* oregano leaves
2 cloves minced garlic
2 tablespoons capers, rinsed
¾ cup extra virgin olive oil
sea salt and fresh pepper to taste

Place ingredients in the blender and puree till well blended.

Yogurt-Poppyseed Dressing

Makes 1½ cups

This dressing is both sweet and tart and would compliment a shrimp or crab salad with ripe summer fruit. Try the dressing as a party dip for fruit kabobs.

   ¾ cup plain Greek yogurt
   1 tablespoon poppyseeds
   1 jalapeno pepper seeded and finely diced
   ½ cup fresh lime juice
   ¼ cup fresh orange juice
   pinch of sea salt and a twist of pepper

Whisk all the ingredients together in a bowl. Season to taste.

Ranch Dressing

Makes about 2 cups

Ranch dressing is an American standard and this tasty recipe will take care of your hankering very nicely. Use it as a raw vegetable dip for parties. You will never buy ranch dressing again after you taste this one.

   1 cup Homemade Mayonnaise
   1 cup plain yogurt (thick Greek yogurt is best)
   1 teaspoon celery seed or 1 tablespoon celery leaves, minced
   4 tablespoons chopped fresh parsley
   4 tablespoons green onion, minced (more if you like)

1 teaspoon fresh oregano, minced (optional)
2 teaspoons minced garlic
2 teaspoons onion powder
juice of ½ lemon
1 teaspoon sea salt & twist of pepper
dash cayenne

Place all ingredients in the blender and puree till smooth. This dressing is best if used within a week. Fresh dressing has *no preservatives*.

Roasted Garlic Vinaigrette

Makes 1⅓ cups

This yummy dressing is a great accompaniment to almost any salad.

4 bulbs roasted garlic, with the garlic squeezed out into a bowl
1½ tablespoons Dijon mustard
¼ cup rice wine vinegar
¾ cup olive oil
sea salt and a twist of pepper

Place the ingredients in the blender and puree until smooth.

Broccoli Rabe and Feta Salad

Serves 6

This salad makes a meal in itself.

> 2 pounds broccoli rabe, bottoms trimmed, cut into 2 inch pieces
> 2 tablespoons lemon juice
> 2 tablespoons Dijon or whole grain mustard
> 1 tablespoon balsamic vinegar
> 4 tablespoons extra virgin olive oil
> ½ cup sliced red onion
> ¼ cup each fresh basil leaves, cilantro and Italian parsley, chopped
> ½ cup pine nuts, toasted
> 6 ounces sheep's milk feta, crumbled
> ¼ teaspoon red pepper flakes
> ½ teaspoon Celtic sea salt, several twists of freshly ground pepper

Garnish: Organic cherry tomatoes, cut in half, Greek Kalamata olives

In a large pot of boiling water, place the asparagus and let it cook for 2–3 minutes until softened and bright green. Drain the broccoli and immediately plunge into ice water.

In a large bowl whisk together the lemon juice, mustard, balsamic, olive oil, red pepper flakes and herbs. Add the cooked broccoli, red onion, feta, pine nuts and salt & pepper. Keep folding all the ingredients together with a wooden spoon or rubber spatula until the ingredients are well combined.

To serve, portion out the salad onto six salad plates. Garnish with more crumbled feta if desired, a drizzle of olive oil and another twist of pepper. Surround the salads with the cherry tomatoes.

Crab and Avocado Salad with Miso Dressing

4 entrée size portions

The dressing in this recipe is so good you will want to use in many other ways. Great as a shrimp dip or a dollop on grilled fish.

For the crab:
>   2 cups cooked Dungeness crab meat
>   juice of 1 lime
>   4 tablespoons mirin (Japanese sweet rice wine)
>   2 tablespoons seasoned rice wine vinegar
>   1 fresh red chile pepper, seeded and finely diced

For the Dressing:
>   Makes about 1¼ cups
>
>   1 cup Homemade Mayonnaise
>   2 tablespoons white miso
>   2 tablespoons mirin (Japanese sweet rice wine)
>   1 tablespoon seasoned rice wine vinegar
>   1 tablespoon San-J *wheat-free* tamari
>   2 cloves minced garlic
>   ¼ teaspoon red pepper flakes
>
>   4 cups arugula or mixed lettuces
>   1 large ripe avocado, pitted and sliced

Garnish: 1 scallion, finely minced, 1 tablespoon crumbled Japanese dried seaweed (optional)

In a bowl whisk the dressing ingredients except for the chile. Remove 2 tablespoons to another large bowl for tossing the greens. Add the crabmeat to the first bowl with the dressing and add the diced chile pepper and mix well with a fork.

In the salad bowl add the lettuces and toss gently coating the leaves well. Place the salad on four plates. Divide the crab mixture in the center of each plate in a mound. Arrange the avocado slices artfully around the crab. Sprinkle some scallion around each salad.

Pass the dressing and let everyone help themselves.

Italian *Caprese* Salad

Serves 6

For this classic Italian salad use *fresh* mozzarella, which has a very creamy texture. Heirloom tomatoes make a beautiful presentation on the plate. For authentic flavor, the tomatoes you use should be just picked from the garden or selected from the farmer's market, although the little organic cherry tomatoes from Mexico (sweet 100's) work very nicely. The better tasting the tomato, the better the salad.

> **1 pint cherry tomatoes (sliced in half lengthwise) or 18 to 24 slices of garden tomato (3–4 slices per salad)**
> **12 ounces (2 ounces per salad) bocconcini (balls) or mozzarella di bufala cheese**
> **½ cup extra virgin olive oil**
> **18 garden fresh basil leaves for garnish**
> **Celtic *Flower of the Sea* salt or Maldon Salt (very light flakes)**
> **Twist of freshly ground pepper**

Arrange the tomatoes on 6 salad plates.

Cut the mozzarella into attractive slices and overlap on the plate with the tomatoes. Drizzle the olive oil evenly over each salad. Arrange the basil leaves on top of each salad. Season with sea salt and a twist of fresh pepper. For a great visual presentation mix the varieties of tomatoes.

Wild Rice and Turkey Salad with Cranberries and Mint

Serves 8

This easy salad is a great way to use leftover Thanksgiving Turkey. It will feed the family the next day so you can relax. This is also a nice buffet salad for a party.

The Salad:

1¼ pounds wild rice, soaked in water overnight and rinsed, then cooked according to package directions.

2 cups leftover turkey, shredded

½ cup toasted hazelnuts, walnuts, pecans or pine nuts

½ cup organic dried cranberries (not sweetened with additional sugar)*

½ cup fresh mint, finely chopped

2 scallions, thinly sliced on the diagonal

8 ounces organic lettuce mix, or other favorite greens

Dressing:

¾ cup extra virgin olive oil

¾ cup fresh organic orange juice

2 tablespoons *microplaned* orange zest

3 tablespoons maple syrup

1 tablespoon Dijon mustard

¼ teaspoon Celtic salt and twist of fresh pepper

In a large bowl whisk together the olive oil, orange juice, orange zest, maple syrup, sea salt and twist of pepper. Add the cooked rice, hazelnuts, cranberries, mint, and scallions. Toss well to mix dressing.

To plate arrange one ounce of the lettuce on each plate. Top with the salad mixture and the shredded turkey. Garnish with additional mint sprigs.

Sauteed Chicken Livers with Summer Greens

Serves 4

This salad could be lunch or dinner.

> **10–12 ounces of organic *range-fed* chicken livers**
> **2 tablespoons KerryGold butter**
> **4 tablespoons extra virgin olive oil**
> **3 tablespoons balsamic vinegar**
> **1 tablespoon lemon juice**
> **½ teaspoon Celtic sea salt & twist of pepper**
> **8 cups favorite summer greens, include some mesclun, arugula and watercress**

Place the chicken livers on a plate and sprinkle with the sea salt and pepper.

In a heavy bottomed skillet heat 2 tablespoons of butter to medium-hot and cook the livers for about 5–7 minutes or until brown on the outside but fairly pink inside. Take the pan off the heat and deglaze with 2 tablespoons of balsamic vinegar. Stir the livers to coat with the vinegar.

In a large bowl place the salad greens. Coat lightly with 4 tablespoons of the extra virgin olive oil, a tablespoon of balsamic vinegar, and the lemon juice. Place the greens on 4 salad plates

Divide the livers onto the salads and spoon extra sauce from the pan over them. Pass the pepper grinder.

Warm Quinoa Salad with Grilled Vegetables and Feta Cheese

Serves 6–8

This salad would be good as a vegetarian entrée. Very hearty! You can also serve the salad with the Lamb Kebabs.

The Quinoa:

2⅓ cups organic quinoa. Soak the quinoa overnight and rinse well.

2 tablespoons cold pressed sesame oil

6 cloves garlic, minced

1 medium red onion, very finely diced

2 large jalapenos, seeded and finely diced

1 teaspoon ground cumin

The Vegetables:

1 pound very fresh asparagus, tough bottoms trimmed

4 Asian eggplants, cut in half lengthwise

4 vine ripe tomatoes, cut in half

2 ripe avocados, pit and skin removed, cut in half

¼ cup cold pressed sesame oil

8 ounces sheep's milk feta, crumbled

¼ cup fresh mint leaves chopped

Dressing:

2 tablespoons balsamic vinegar

2 tablespoons fresh lemon juice

4 tablespoons extra virgin olive oil

1 teaspoon red pepper flakes

pinch sea salt & twist of pepper to taste

Garnish: 1 cup Greek Kalamata olives, your favorite greens, (arugula would be nice), toasted pine nuts and sprigs of mint.

After rinsing the quinoa, place in a 4 quart saucepan and cover with lightly salted water. Cook for about 15 minutes or until fluffy and dry. Remove cooked quinoa to a large bowl to cool, fluffing with fork.

In a heavy bottomed skillet, over medium heat, heat 4 tablespoons of the oil. Add the garlic and cook until fragrant, add the onion and jalapenos and cook until soft, about 5 minutes. Add the cumin and stir well. Transfer the mixture to the quinoa and mix well.

For the grilled vegetables, prepare the grill to medium hot. Place the vegetables on a sheetpan and brush liberally with 4 tablespoons of oil. Grill the asparagus, avocadoes & tomatoes for about 5 minutes, the eggplant for 10 minutes. Remove the vegetables to a cutting board and cut into attractive bite size pieces.

To serve the salad, place a bed of greens on a large platter. Top with the cooked quinoa and arrange the grilled vegetables on top. Garnish with the crumbled feta cheese, the Kalamata olives, the toasted pine nuts and the mint.

Whisk together the olive oil, balsamic vinegar, lemon juice and the red pepper flakes and pour over the salad. Give the salad a few twists of black pepper.

Barbecued Chicken Salad

Serves 6

This salad is a simple, quick to make meal when you have leftover chicken. You can also use any other choice of lettuces that you fancy. Leftover steak will also work for this salad. This is a family friendly recipe.

The Dressing:
> 1 clove of garlic, minced
> 1 teaspoon Dijon mustard
> 3 tablespoons red wine vinegar
> 1 teaspoon fresh thyme leaves
> dash Worcestershire
> dash Tabasco
> ¾ cup extra virgin olive oil
> sea salt and fresh pepper to taste

In a medium bowl, whisk together all the ingredients and set aside.

The Salad:
> 2 cups leftover roasted chicken, shredded
> 2 stalks celery, finely diced
> 1 red onion, finely diced
> ½ cup Mediterranean or English cucumber, seeded and diced
> ¼ cup toasted pecans, chopped
> ¾ cup grated grass-fed New Zealand grass-fed cheddar or raw milk cheddar
> 2 carrots, grated
> ½ head Napa cabbage thinly sliced

1 cup radicchio thinly sliced
6 tablespoons Grilled Tomato Catsup or barbeque sauce
sea salt & freshly ground pepper

Garnish: ½ cup cilantro leaves 12–16 organic cherry tomatoes, cut in half

Place the shredded chicken in a large bowl. Add the diced celery, red onion, cucumber, toasted pecans, grated carrots, Napa cabbage, radicchio and the Grilled Tomato Catsup. Sprinkle the ingredients with a little sea salt and a twist of pepper and mix gently and thoroughly.

To serve arrange the salad ingredients on 6 plates. Whisk the dressing again and spoon liberally over each salad. Garnish with the cilantro and cherry tomato halves.

Savory Green Salad

Serves 4

This is a good every day salad with big taste and lots of interest.

Savory Salad:
> 4 cups savory greens, such as watercress, arugula, mizuna or microgreens
> Sprouted radish or sunflower seeds
> Toasted Goat Cheese rounds or a good blue cheese (Maytag Blue Cheese or Pt. Reyes Original Blue)
> Pecan halves or chopped walnuts

Savory Dressing:
> In a bowl, whisk together
> 1 tablespoon minced shallot
> 2 tablespoons Spanish Sherry vinegar
> 1 tablespoon balsamic vinegar
> ¼ cup extra virgin olive oil
> 1 tablespoon lemon juice
> pinch sea salt & a twist of pepper

In a small bowl whisk together the dressing.

In a large bowl toss the greens with the dressing. Arrange the greens on four salad plates. Sprinkle with the sprouts. Top with the cheese. Garnish with the pecans or walnuts. Serve and pass the pepper grinder.

Grapefruit Salad with Microgreens and Herbs

Serves 4

This salad is wonderfully refreshing. For an entree you can add some cooked shrimp or Dungeness crab.

> 1 large 1¾-pound red grapefruit
> 1 large 1¾-pound white grapefruit
> ½ cup fresh mint leaves preferably from the garden
> 1 cup fresh tarragon leaves, taken off the stem
> ½ cup *very fresh* basil leaves
> 1 scallion, finely minced
> 4 tablespoons extra virgin olive oil
> 6 tablespoons grapefruit juice
> pinch sea salt and twist of pepper

Garnish: ⅔ cup microgreens. Avocado slices (optional)

Peel and segment the grapefruit by cutting between the sections with a sharp knife. Reserve 6 tablespoons of the juice.

In a small bowl whisk together the grapefruit juice, olive oil, salt and pepper. Set aside.

Wash the herbs and gently pat dry. Stack the basil leaves, roll into a cigar shape and slice very thin. This is called a chiffonade. In a bowl combine all the herbs (but not the microgreens) and minced chives.

To serve, Place the herbs on 4 salad plates. Divide the grapefruit sections onto the herbs. Spoon some dressing on top of each salad and garnish the top of the salads with the microgreens and avocado.

Seafood Salad with Mangoes, Avocado and Meyer Lemon Vinaigrette

Serves 4 as an entrée

This fresh and lovely composed salad has two complimentary dressings. You could also use slices of sashimi grade tuna instead of the crab or shrimp.

> 1-ripe, firm mango, peeled, seeded and diced
> 1 large ripe avocado, peeled and diced
> 12 ounces (total weight), lightly cooked Dungeness crab or shrimp
> 8 ounces (total) baby arugula, watercress or red oak leaf lettuces
> zest of 2 limes

Tamari-Ginger Dressing:
> ½ cup Homemade Mayonnaise
> 1 teaspoon *microplaned* ginger
> 1 teaspoon Nama Shoyu soy sauce or San-J *wheat free* tamari
> 2 tablespoons Meyer lemon juice
> (or 1 tablespoon regular lemon juice and 1 tablespoon fresh orange juice)

Meyer Lemon Vinaigrette:
> zest of 1 Meyer lemon
> 2 tablespoons Meyer lemon juice (or 1 tablespoon lemon juice and 1 tablespoon fresh orange juice)
> ¼ cup extra virgin olive oil
> ¼ teaspoon sea salt
> twist of freshly ground pepper

For the Dressing: In a small bowl mix all the dressing ingredients. Cover and chill until used.

For the Vinaigrette: In a small bowl whisk together the lemon juice, zest, salt and pepper. Slowly whisk in the olive oil. Set aside.

For the Salad: In a medium bowl place the seafood and blend in 2 tablespoons of the vinaigrette.

In another bowl gently toss the salad greens, the diced mangoes, avocado, and the lime zest with the remaining vinaigrette. To plate the salads divide the mango-lettuce mixture onto four plates, then top with the seafood mixture. Dot some of the Tamari-Ginger Dressing on the salads or serve it on the side.

Caesar Salad

Serves 8

This dressing is one of my standards from catering days. For a variation, if you don't like anchovies, you can use horseradish. The dressing makes a fantastic dip for vegetables or shrimp at a party. It's also great on grilled vegetables. I love to have Caesar dressing in the refrigerator for a quick lunch. For an entrée salad, use 2–3 ounces of cooked chicken, seafood, or steak per person. For non-gluten croutons use Lydia's Sunflower Seed Bread, or make your own croutons from the *everydayraw* cookbook by Mathew Kenny or the *I Am Grateful* raw food cookbook.

> 2 heads of pre-washed organic romaine lettuce
> 1¼ cups extra virgin olive oil
> ¼ cup red wine vinegar
> 1 tablespoon lemon juice
> 3 large egg yolks
> 1 teaspoon minced garlic
> 1 tablespoon Dijon mustard
> 1 tablespoon Worcestershire sauce
> 3 tablespoons anchovy paste (in tube) or 3–4 tablespoons creamed horseradish
> 3 tablespoons Parmesan cheese, grated
> pinch sea salt and a twist of pepper

Whisk together the oil, lemon juice and vinegar in a large measuring cup. Combine the remaining ingredients in a blender. While blender is running, slowly add the oil, lemon juice and vinegar until mixture is emulsified. Taste dressing and adjust flavors to your taste.

For the salad, chop the desired amount of the pre-washed and chilled romaine lettuce leaves, the colder the better. Place the lettuce in a large bowl and add the required amount of dressing to coat the lettuce well. Plate the salads and serve immediately. Garnish with more grated Parmesan and twists of pepper.

Colorful Cobb Salad

Serves 4

Cobb salad makes a substantial meal and you can use steak, chicken or seafood to suit your preference. This salad will please your family or guests for a Sunday luncheon.

8 ounces cooked steak, chicken, or seafood cut into ½ inch cubes
4 hardboiled eggs, peeled and quartered
1 cup crumbled Maytag Blue or Pt. Reyes Blue or another blue cheese of your choice
1½ cup diced avocado
1½ cups peeled and diced ripe red or yellow tomatoes, or organic cherry tomatoes cut in half
12 grilled or roasted scallions, room temperature, chopped
8 cups mesclun mix or other favorite lettuces

Garnish: 4 tablespoons chopped chives (1-inch pieces)

The Dressing:
1 minced shallot
⅓ cup lemon juice
1 cup extra virgin olive oil
2 tablespoons minced chives
pinch of sea salt and a twist of pepper

Whisk the first 4 dressing ingredients together in a bowl. Season to taste and set aside.

In another bowl toss the tomatoes in 2 tablespoons of the dressing. In a large bowl toss the greens in ½ of the dressing.

To serve arrange the lettuce on 4 dinner plates and then lay out the remaining salad ingredients in rows. Drizzle the salad with the remaining dressing and garnish with the chives. Pass the pepper grinder.

Beef Carpaccio Salad with Cornichon Vinaigrette

Serves 6

This recipe would work equally well with paper-thin slices of roast turkey breast or smoked salmon.

> **18 ounces** *grass-fed* **beef tenderloin**
> **3 hardboiled eggs, quartered**
> **¾ cup radishes, minced**
> **3 tablespoons capers, rinsed and chopped**
> **3 tablespoons cornichons, minced**
> **3 tablespoons fresh chives, chopped**
> **3 tablespoons fresh lemon juice**
> **½ teaspoon sea salt & twist of black pepper**
> **7 tablespoons extra virgin olive oil**
> **6 ounces baby arugula**
> **4 tablespoons** *microplaned* **Parmesan cheese**

Wrap the beef in plastic, and chill in freezer until firm, about 1 hour. Using a very sharp knife, cut beef across the grain into ⅛-inch thick slices. Gently pound slices between pieces of waxed paper. Refrigerate beef slices between pieces of waxed paper for 1–2 hours.

Force the hard boiled eggs through a fine sieve into a small bowl. Add radishes, capers, cornichons, and chives to eggs and then mix very gently.

In a medium bowl, whisk together the lemon juice, salt, and pepper. Slowly add the olive oil in a thin stream whisking until the ingredients are emulsified.

To plate, arrange the beef carpaccio onto four large plates. Drizzle all but 2 tablespoons vinaigrette over the meat, then sprinkle with the egg/cornichon mixture.

Add the arugula to the bowl with the remaining 2 tablespoons of dressing and toss with the 4 tablespoons of Parmesan cheese. Mound the salad in the center of each plate on top of the meat. Pass the pepper grinder if desired.

Japanese Salad with White Miso Vinaigrette

Serves 6

White Miso is very mild and slightly sweet. This is a very nourishing entrée salad.

    18 ounces shredded cooked chicken, seafood or rare steak
    3 tablespoons organic white miso paste
    2–3 tablespoons seasoned rice wine vinegar
    1 tablespoon pickled ginger
    2 carrots cut into matchsticks
    1 head radicchio, thinly sliced
    2–3 scallions thinly sliced on the diagonal
    2 sheets nori, cut into thin strips (optional)

Garnish: 2–3 tablespoons toasted sesame seeds

In a large bowl, whisk together the miso with the sesame oil, rice wine vinegar, and 3 tablespoons warm water. Add the cooked meat or seafood, carrots, green onion, pickled ginger, and nori strips. Toss well.

To serve, place the thinly sliced radicchio on the salad plates. Divide the salad mixture onto each plate. Garnish the salads with the toasted sesame seeds.

Green Goddess Salad

Serves 8

Green Goddess dressing is as delicious as it is beautiful. Use it on cold cooked vegetables as well as salad. This salad will make a meal.

Salad Ingredients:

8 ounces favorite salad greens, romaine, frisee, arugula, mesclun or oak leaf

3 ounces, per person, cooked chicken, steak or seafood

2–3 Persian cucumbers or 1 English cucumber, sliced lengthwise & then on the diagonal

1 basket organic cherry tomatoes, cut in half

½ cup radishes, thinly sliced

Arrange the greens, vegetables and chicken, steak or seafood attractively on large size plates. Spoon the dressing over the salads.

Green Goddess Dressing:

Makes about 2 cups

½ ripe avocado

1 large clove of garlic, minced

2 tablespoons anchovy paste

1 large scallion, chopped

2 tablespoons each fresh tarragon and cilantro leaves

1 tablespoon fresh basil leaves

3 tablespoons Italian flat leaf parsley

2 teaspoons each lemon juice and lime juice

3 tablespoons white wine vinegar

¾ cup extra virgin olive oil

¼ cup whipping cream
sea salt and fresh pepper

In the food processor, puree all the ingredients except the olive oil and whipping cream. With the motor running slowly add the olive oil until well incorporated. Remove ingredients to a bowl and whisk in the cream and season with salt and pepper to taste.

Lamb Salad with Thai Dressing

Serves 4

This is another great salad and you can use the same Thai Dressing.

12 ounces leftover roast leg of lamb, preferably rare, or use steak
2 tablespoons extra virgin olive oil
4 cups of your favorite greens
1 scallion, sliced on the diagonal
3 tablespoons chopped fresh mint

Garnish: ¼ cup chopped macadamia nuts, or toasted pine nuts

In a large frying pan heat the oil over medium heat. Toss in the meat to warm slightly. Season with a pinch of sea salt.

In a large bowl place the greens, scallion and the mint. Toss the greens in some of the Thai dressing. Place the greens on four salad plates. Place the warmed lamb on top, then the macadamia nuts. Add a little more of the dressing.

Mediterranean Spinach and Feta Salad with Lemon-Coriander Marinated Olives

Serves 6

This classic salad is very fast to make. It is even more special with the use of the Coriander Marinated Olives. Greek Kalamata olives will also work very well with this salad.

The Olives:

> Marinate for 8 hours or overnight
> ½ pound cracked, but not pitted, Cypriot or cerignola olives
> ¼ cup extra virgin olive oil
> ⅛ cup fresh lemon juice (use Meyer lemons if possible)
> 3–4 cloves of garlic, crushed
> 1 tablespoon whole cracked coriander seeds
> ½ lemon, cut into small wedges
> 1 fresh or dried bay leaf cut into quarters

In a glass bowl combine all the ingredients. Cover and refrigerate for at least 8 hours, stirring occasionally. Olives will keep for a month. Bring olives to room temperature before serving.

The Salad:

> 12 ounces baby spinach leaves
> 6 ounces sheep's milk feta cheese, crumbled
> juice of one lemon
> 6 tablespoons extra virgin olive oil
> pinch of sea salt and fresh pepper to taste

2–3 ripe organic tomatoes cut into wedges or 1 cup organic cherry tomatoes cut in half
2–3 small Persian cucumbers sliced on the diagonal
1 red onion skin, removed and sliced very thin into rings

Garnish: The olives and additional lemon wedges

In a large bowl place the spinach and the feta cheese. In another small bowl, whisk together the lemon juice and the olive oil. Season with the sea salt and pepper to taste. Pour the dressing over the spinach/cheese mixture and mix very well until the cheese and dressing coat the leaves.

To serve plate the salads and garnish with the tomatoes, red onion rings cucumbers, olives and the additional lemon wedges, if desired. Pass the pepper grinder.

Mexican Steak Salad with Chipotle Chile Dressing

Serves 4

Chipotle chiles are hot and smoky. You may add more to this recipe if you like the heat turned up.

1 pound grass-fed flank steak
1 large red onion sliced thick into rings
Celtic sea salt and freshly ground pepper
Sesame oil for grilling
4 large garden tomatoes cut in half, brushed with sesame oil
1 large head of romaine

Garnish: ½ cup chopped cilantro, ½ cup toasted pumpkinseeds, or pine nuts

In a bowl mix the onion slices with some sesame oil to coat, season with salt and pepper. Brush the sesame oil on both sides of the flank steak. Grill over hot fire rare to medium rare. At the same time place the tomatoes, cut side down on the grill and cook until well seared.

When the steak and tomatoes are done remove and let stand 5 minutes to rest. Slice the steak thin and arrange the steak over a platter of chopped romaine lettuce. Garnish with the chopped cilantro and toasted pumpkin seeds. Place the grilled tomatoes around the edge. Drizzle the salad with some of the Chipotle dressing and pass the rest.

Chipotle Chile Dressing:
    1 cup organic sour cream
    juice of one lime
    1 teaspoon minced garlic
    1 "canned" chipotle chile in adobo sauce
    pinch sea salt and twist of pepper

Blend the ingredients together in the food processor or blender. Check for balance of flavors. Set aside.

Thai Salad with Spicy Dressing

Serves 6

This salad is a whole meal. The dressing is exceptional and is also good as a marinade. You can prepare the salad, as described below, or you could offer all the ingredients in separate bowls, buffet style, and let your guests have the fun of creating their own salads.

The Salad Ingredients:
 ½ head Napa cabbage, shredded
 2 cups chopped, cooked, chicken or seafood
 2 bell peppers (red, yellow, or orange) cut into matchsticks
 2 large carrots cut into matchsticks
 1 bunch green onion, thinly sliced on the diagonal
 1 cup halved organic cherry tomatoes
 1 cup mung bean sprouts
 enoki or other fresh sliced mushrooms (optional)
 1 cup roasted macadamia nuts, finely chopped
 1 cup chopped cilantro leaves

In a large bowl toss the shredded cabbage in some of the dressing. Arrange the cabbage on a large platter. Scatter the cooked chicken or seafood on top of the cabbage. Artistically arrange the prepared bell peppers, carrots, green onions, and tomatoes around the edge of the salad, and scatter the mung bean sprouts on top. Whisk the dressing and spoon some more evenly over top.

Garnish the salad with ½ cup of the chopped macadamias and the cilantro. Pass more dressing, if desired.

Spicy Dressing:

Makes about 3 cups

¾ cup seasoned rice wine vinegar
1 cup organic cold pressed sesame oil
¼ cup Nama Shoyu soy sauce or San-J *wheat-free* tamari
juice of one lime (more if you like)
2 tablespoons minced garlic
4 tablespoons *microplaned* fresh or frozen ginger* (see note)
1 teaspoon red pepper flakes
1 jalapeno pepper, seeded and finely diced

In a bowl whisk together all the dressing ingredients. This dressing keeps really well in the refrigerator.

*Note: Keep fresh ginger in the freezer. It grates easily when it's frozen. Refreeze immediately.

Chicken Sausage Salad

Serves 2

I made this quick salad one day when I was visiting my daughter Shannon and her husband Anthony in the Bay Area.

2 organic Bruce Aidells or AmyLu chicken sausages, chopped
2 tablespoons cold pressed sesame oil
2 large handfuls organic spinach leaves
1 tablespoon balsamic vinegar
1 tablespoon lemon juice
2 ounces Sheep's milk feta, crumbled feta
2 large handfuls favorite lettuces, placed on your salad plates

Garnish: Drizzle of extra virgin olive oil, ½ cup organic cherry tomatoes halves, Persian cucumber slices, some favorite olives and toasted pine nuts.

In a large skillet heat the oil to medium-hot. Place the chopped sausage in the pan and begin to brown. Add the 2 handfuls of spinach and begin to wilt. Add the lemon juice and balsamic and toss well. Turn the salad out onto two plates and top with the crumbled feta.

Garnish the salads with the drizzle of olive oil, cherry tomatoes, cucumber, olives and toasted pine nuts. A couple grinds of fresh pepper is perfect.

"Pastured" Egg Salad

Serves 4

Egg salad is a childhood favorite. Serve the egg salad on a bed of lightly dressed lettuces with some beautiful olives.

> **8 *pastured* eggs, if you can find some, otherwise use organic *free-range* eggs**
> **⅓ cup Homemade Mayonnaise**
> **3 scallions, white and light green parts, thinly sliced**
> **1 tablespoon each, tarragon and parsley**
> **1 tablespoon Dijon or whole grain mustard**
> **squeeze of lemon juice, or to taste**
> **pinch sea salt and a twist of pepper**
> **dash cayenne**
> **4 cups favorite lettuces**

Garnish: 1 tablespoon chopped chives, thinly sliced radishes and some special olives.

Place the eggs in a saucepan of cold water and bring to a boil. Boil for 2 minutes and then turn off the heat. Cover the pan and let the eggs sit for about 6 minutes. Place the eggs in cold water to cool then peel.

In a bowl smash the eggs with a fork. Add the mayonnaise, scallion, tarragon, parsley, mustard, lemon juice, salt, pepper and cayenne. Mix well and taste for seasonings. Add more mayonnaise, if necessary.

Place the greens in a bowl and toss with 2 tablespoons extra virgin olive oil to coat.

To plate the salads mound the greens onto 4 dinner plates. Spoon the egg salad into the center of each mound. Garnish with the chopped chives, radishes and olives.

Condiments
and Sauces

Homemade sauces and condiments are not only healthier, they are much tastier than store bought, which normally contain ingredients to be avoided. At home I make a variety of sauces and condiments and since I live with people who's tastes vary, we set these choices out at dinner so everyone can select what they want.

Very Rich and Spicy Tomato Sauce

Makes about 3 quarts

This rich tomato sauce is my version of the tomato sauce that one of my catering clients from Florence, Italy used to make. She would make huge batches of the sauce every summer with tomatoes from her garden. You can use this sauce when you make meatballs, or use it as a sauce for grilled chicken or fish.

¼ cup extra virgin olive oil
1 large onion, minced
1 leeks, trimmed and minced (rinsed of any grit)
3 celery ribs, trimmed and minced
2 carrots, peeled and minced
1 bulb garlic, peeled and minced
2 jalapeno peppers seeded and minced
1 teaspoon red pepper flakes
3 pounds fresh garden tomatoes, peeled, seeded and chopped
½ cup fresh basil leaves, chopped
2 tablespoons fresh oregano leaves, chopped
½ cup dry red wine
1 tablespoon honey
1 cube of KerryGold butter, cut into small pieces
½ cup organic whipping cream
sea salt and fresh pepper to taste

In a heavy bottomed pot heat the oil to medium-high. Add the onions, leeks, carrots and garlic and sauté until very caramelized and brown. Add the jalepenos and red pepper flakes and cook for one minute more.

Add the tomatoes, herbs, red wine and honey and reduce heat to a simmer. Cook slowly for about 1 to 1½ hours. Towards the end of the cooking time whisk in the butter, whipping cream salt and pepper. Cook for another 30 minutes to incorporate flavors. Remove from heat.

When the mixture cools you can puree it in the food processor and strain the solids out for a smoother sauce if you prefer. I think its fine just the way it is. This is my favorite tomato sauce.

"Very Green" Herb Sauce

Makes about 3 cups

This is a vibrant sauce for grilled chicken or fish. It's also a very pretty dip for raw party vegetables.

> 2 tablespoons organic apricot fruit puree (no added sugar)
> 4 cloves garlic, chopped
> 2 scallions, finely chopped
> 1½ cups cilantro leaves, no stems
> ½ cup basil leaves
> ½ cup parsley leaves
> ½ cup tarragon (optional)
> ½ pine nuts
> ¼ cup lemon juice
> 1 cup cold pressed sesame oil
> pinch of cayenne pepper
> sea salt & twist of pepper to taste

Place all ingredients except for oil in the food processor. With the motor running gradually add the oil until the mixture is thick and creamy.

Tapenade

Yields approximately 3 cups

This traditional French condiment is great on grilled fish or meats. Use it with raw vegetables for a party.

   3 cups pitted Kalamata or Nicoise olives
   2 tablespoons capers, rinsed
   1 tablespoon anchovy paste or 2 salt-packed anchovies
   ½ cup toasted pine nuts or walnuts, finely chopped
   1 garlic clove
   1 tablespoon fresh basil, chopped
   1 tablespoon fresh flat leaf parsley, chopped
   extra virgin olive oil as needed
   Pinch of cayenne or twist of black pepper

Place all the ingredients, except the olive oil in the bowl of the food processor. With the motor running drizzle the olive oil into the mixture until everything is smooth. Add a pinch of sea salt if necessary.

Thanksgiving Cranberry Chutney

This is the *best cranberry sauce* ever as it is redolent with fragrant spices. Give it as a Christmas gift in a small Mason jar with a plaid ribbon. For one of the best sandwiches ever try a turkey sandwich on homemade cornbread with the cranberry chutney. Incredible!

1 lemon
1½ cups water
½ cup organic apricot fruit puree or cooked and pureed dried apricots (unsulphered)
½ cup raw honey
½ cup Bragg's apple cider vinegar
1 teaspoon curry powder
¼ teaspoon ground cloves
1 cinnamon stick or ½ teaspoon ground cinnamon
2 medium organic granny smith apples, cored, peeled and chopped
3 cups fresh or frozen organic cranberries
1 cup organic golden raisins
½ cup chopped pecans or walnuts

In a small saucepan blanch lemon in water for 2 minutes. When cool, seed and chop.

In a large *stainless steel* (do not use aluminum) saucepan, combine the water, jam, vinegar, honey and the spices and bring to a boil, stirring until the honey is dissolved.

Reduce the heat and add the chopped apples and lemon and cook for 10 minutes. Then add the cranberries and the raisins and simmer for another 25 minutes, uncovered, until thick. Stir often to prevent scorching. Remove from heat and add the nuts.

Garlic Aioli

Aioli is a luxurious, very garlicky sauce for steamed or grilled vegetables. You can use it instead of store bought mayonnaise. For a variation use roasted *garlic* to make the aioli. Roasting the garlic adds mellowness.

> 6 cloves of garlic
> 2 tablespoons sherry vinegar
> 2 eggs
> 1 tablespoon Dijon mustard
> ½ cup extra virgin olive oil
> ½ cup cold pressed sesame oil
> 1 teaspoon sea salt and a twist of fresh pepper

Place all the ingredients except the oils in the blender. Turn the blender on low to start, then turn it up to high and slowly add the oils until they emulsify. Taste and adjust the seasonings. You can substitute lemon for the sherry vinegar. You can also add herbs like tarragon or if you want a spicy aioli add some chopped jalapenos.

Grilled Tomato Ketchup

Makes about 1 cup

Making your very own ketchup is fun.

> Grill or broil until charred:
> 4 ripe Roma tomatoes (whole)
> 1 small red onion, peeled and halved
> 1 whole, large jalapeno pepper. Remove seeds and stem after grilling

Combine the above in the food processor with:

2 tablespoons apple cider vinegar
1 tablespoon raw honey
**1 tablespoon Dijon or whole grain mustard, or creamed horse-
radish**
1 tablespoon fresh lime or lemon juice

Place all the ingredients in the food processor with the metal blade. Pulse the machine off and on until the sauce is chopped and has a chunky look. At this point you can add ¼ cup cilantro leaves if you like.

Mexican Mole

Moles originate from Puebla, Mexico. Traditionally there were seven moles, each with different nuts, seeds and spices. Families guarded their particular recipe and would go to a shop where there were special grinding machines to grind all the ingredients together into a paste. You can use the mole as a sauce for chicken or holiday turkey, if you really want a very unusual feast. I like to spread mole on my sprouted corn tortilla when making enchiladas or tacos.

¼ cup pine nuts or chopped almonds
¼ cup sesame seeds
3 Ezekiel sprouted corn tortillas
2–3 dried chiles negros
5 ancho chiles
¼ cup cold pressed sesame oil
½ small onion, diced
3–4 cloves garlic, diced
2 serrano chiles, stemmed and seeded
1 apple, peeled, cored and chopped
½ organic banana, peeled and chopped
4 organic plum tomatoes
¼ cup organic raisins or golden raisins
2–3 cups chicken or vegetable broth
½ teaspoon cinnamon
6 sprigs of fresh oregano leaves
2 ounces organic super dark 73% chocolate, Trader Joe's is good

Toast the pine nuts and sesame seeds in a skillet. Set aside. Toast the corn tortillas in the skillet until brown. Tear into pieces. Set aside.

Remove stems and seeds from the dried chilies. Place the chiles on a sheet pan and toast in the oven (350) for 3 to 5 minutes, or until fragrant. Do not let them get too dark. Then cover the chiles, in a bowl with warm water until they soften, about 10 minutes. Then puree the chiles in the blender with the broth.

In a large skillet heat the oil. Add the onions, garlic, serrano chiles and apple and cook until brown. Add the banana and the plum tomatoes, then the pureed chiles, pine nut sesame seed mix, raisins, torn tortillas, cinnamon, oregano and chocolate. Simmer mixture over low heat for about 20 minutes.

Transfer the mixture, in batches, to the blender and puree until very smooth. You may need to add a little more broth. For a more refined sauce strain the mixture through a sieve. The mole can be made a day or two ahead and refrigerated. You can also freeze it.

Eat Your Vegetables!

Grilled or Roasted Asparagus

Serves 4

Grilling or roasting adds a special flavor to asparagus.

One bunch *really fresh* **asparagus**

Dressing:
> **½ cup balsamic vinegar**
> **½ cup extra virgin olive oil**
> **1 clove garlic, minced**
> **Celtic sea salt, freshly ground pepper**

Whisk together the dressing and set aside.

Place the asparagus on a clean, hot grill, brush with a little olive oil and turn until slightly browned on all sides. Asparagus should still be somewhat crisp. When done place asparagus on a platter and drizzle with the dressing. At this point you can crumble some fresh goat cheese on top or freshly grated Parmesan. Season with Celtic sea salt and a twist of pepper.

*To roast asparagus, place in a glass baking dish, brushed with a little oil. Bake in a hot 450 degree oven turning frequently until evenly browned.

Sautéed Broccoli Rabe with Parmesan

Serves 6

Broccoli rabe is more expensive than regular broccoli, but it is very tender and delicious, so it's well worth it for this dish.

Two 12 ounce bunches broccoli rabe
4 tablespoons cold pressed sesame oil
½ small onion, cut in half and thinly sliced
4 cloves garlic, minced
½ teaspoon red chile flakes
1 pint organic "sweet 100's" cherry tomatoes, from Mexico
4 tablespoons toasted pecans, chopped
Celtic sea salt & a twist of pepper

Garnish: grated Parmesan cheese

In a large skillet, heat 2 tablespoons of the oil, add the onion, garlic & chile flakes and sauté until onion is caramelized.

Cut about 1" off the bottom of the broccoli rabe. Then add the broccoli rabe to the skillet. Add 2 tablespoons water and put a lid on the skillet. Cook until the broccoli is tender but still bright green. Remove broccoli to a warm platter.

In the same pan add 2 tablespoons of the oil and cook the cherry tomatoes, stirring occasionally until the skin splits.

Spoon the tomatoes on top of the broccoli rabe and sprinkle on the toasted pecans. Season with Celtic sea salt and a twist of fresh pepper.

Garnish with the Parmesan cheese and drizzle some extra virgin olive oil on top.

Sautéed Greens

Serves 6

I eat sautéed kale or chard at least three nights a week. I use onions, lots of garlic and red bell pepper to add flavor and color. Onions and garlic are good antioxidants and this recipe is a very tasty way to get your family to eat their greens.

> **2 bunches organic kale, Swiss chard, mustard greens or spinach (you can mix them up)**
> **2 tablespoons cold pressed sesame oil**
> **6 cloves garlic, minced**
> **1 medium yellow onion, sliced thin**
> **1 red bell pepper, seeded and sliced**
> **½ teaspoon sea salt & a twist of fresh pepper**
> **juice of ½ lemon or 1 tablespoon of balsamic vinegar**
> **¼ teaspoon red pepper flakes (optional)**

Wash the greens and tear the leaves off the stems.

In a large sauté skillet heat the oil. Sauté the onions until nicely browned and crispy. Then add the garlic, sliced red bell pepper and the greens. Season and toss everything well. I add one or two tablespoons of water to the pan and put a lid on the vegetables and let them steam until the greens are just wilted but still bright green. You don't want to overcook the greens. I like the bell pepper a little on the crunchy side too.

To serve, whisk together the lemon juice or balsamic with 2 tablespoons of extra virgin olive oil and the red pepper flakes. Toss the greens, again, like a salad, and turn out onto a warm platter or just serve them from the pan.

Haricots Verts Nicoise

Serves 6

I love these little delicate French green beans the best. This is a classic preparation which is served at room temperature, so it's perfect for the picnic or barbecue. The haricots verts will make a nice accompaniment to a simply prepared chicken or fish.

> **1 pound French green beans or any young garden bean (bush or pole)**
> **1 pint organic cherry tomatoes, (sweet 100's), halved**
> **1 tablespoon extra virgin olive oil**
> **½ cup pitted Nicoise olives**
> **¼ cup toasted pine nuts**

Blanch the beans in salted water for 2–3 minutes. You will want them al dente and bright green. Drain the beans and set aside on a platter to cool. In a bowl, just before serving, toss the beans with the olive oil, tomatoes and Nicoise olives.

Arrange the beans on individual salad plates or just put them in an attractive bowl and sprinkle the toasted pine nuts on top. Pass the pepper grinder.

Roasted Winter Vegetables

Serves 6

The winter vegetables make a very heartwarming dish when the weather is cold. Serve the vegetables with the Bagna Cauda Sauce or the Garlic Aioli.

> 1 cauliflower head
> 6 small fennel bulbs
> 15–16 baby carrots
> 1 acorn squash
> ½ pound broccoli flowerettes or broccoli rabe
> 1 head Belgian endive
> 1 head radicchio or Traviso
> Celtic *Flower of the Ocean* sea salt

Bring to a boil a large pot of salted water.

Cut the cauliflower into bite size pieces. Cut the acorn squash in half and scoop out the seeds. Then cut the squash into 1" sections. Trim the broccoli into small flowerettes. Cut the fennel into wedge shaped pieces, keeping the root end intact. Peel the baby carrots leaving about ¼" of stem. Cut the carrots in half lengthwise.

Blanch the vegetables, one at a time, beginning with the cauliflower, then the fennel, then carrots and then broccoli. Cook until just done, but still crisp. Lift the vegetables out of the pot with a slotted spoon or tongs. Plunge into ice water to stop the cooking and then remove the vegetable to a waiting platter. Bring the water in the pot back to a boil each time you add another vegetable.

Heat 4 tablespoons of butter in a large sauté pan. Add the cooked and drained vegetables to the pan, stirring gently and heating the vegetables thoroughly. At this point you can place the vegetables on a stainless steel sheet pan and roast them in a 400 degree oven until lightly browned. Either way will work.

Arrange the Belgian endive and radicchio attractively on 6 salad plates. Then arrange the warmed vegetables on top.

Sprinkle the vegetables with a little Celtic *Flower of the Ocean* sea salt and a twist of fresh pepper. Garnish with fresh sprigs of thyme if you have it. These vegetables would be a nice accompaniment to chicken or fish or with quinoa.

Italian Peppers with Capers

Serves 4

I love colorful peppers. This is a simple, rustic side dish to be served with grilled fish, chicken, lamb kebobs or flank steak.

> ¼ cup extra virgin olive oil
> 2 large sweet onions, sliced thin
> 2 yellow or orange bell peppers, sliced thin
> 2 red bell peppers, sliced thin
> 3 ripe tomatoes, peeled and chopped or one pint organic cherry tomatoes cut in half
> 1 tablespoon red wine or balsamic vinegar
> ¼ cup *salt-cured* or regular capers, rinsed

In a large saucepan over medium heat, warm the olive oil. Add the onions and sauté until golden brown, 6–8 minutes. Add the peppers and tomatoes and cook for 4–5 minutes, until the liquid has evaporated and the peppers are soft. If you are using the cherry tomatoes, cook the peppers first and add the cherry tomatoes at the end so they don't break down. Remove from the heat and add the vinegar, and capers. Mix well. Serve at room temperature.

Spaghetti Squash Gratin

Serves 6–8

Spaghetti squash is fun. The gratin would make a good Thanksgiving side dish as a replacement for the overly sweet baked yams with marshmallows. One day I had some ground nuts left from baking a tart and I sprinkled them on the top of the gratin before baking. The nuts really dressed it up.

2 pounds spaghetti squash, cut in half lengthwise.

Pre-bake the squash at 350.

Place the squash, *cut side down*, on a foil lined sheet pan, sprayed with vegetable oil. Bake the squash for about 40 minutes, or until fork tender. Remove from the oven, scoop out the seeds first and then scoop the pulp evenly into a buttered oval gratin dish.

2 tablespoons KerryGold butter
2 cups onions, thinly sliced
3–4 cloves garlic, minced
2 cups vegetable or chicken broth
1 tablespoon fresh thyme, chopped
½ cup heavy cream
1 cup grated Gruyere or Swiss cheese
sea salt and freshly ground pepper to taste
2 tablespoons minced parsley

In a large skillet, sauté the onions and garlic in the butter, 6–8 minutes until light brown. Add the vegetable broth, salt & pepper ant thyme and bring to a boil. Pour the onion-broth over the squash and bake for 30 minutes. Then drizzle the cream over the top of the squash and arrange the grated cheese on top. Return the gratin to the oven and bake until the top is brown and bubbly. Just before serving sprinkle the parsley on top.

Broccoli, Sicilian Style

Serves 8

2 pounds broccoli, cut into florets (you can use broccolini)
4 tablespoons cold pressed sesame oil
3 medium onion, thinly sliced
½ cup Zinfandel
2 tablespoons red wine vinegar
4 sprigs Italian flat leaf parsley
½ teaspoon fresh oregano
4 cloves garlic, thinly sliced
¼ teaspoon red chile flakes
1 tablespoon organic tomato paste
One 28 ounce can organic plum tomatoes, crushed, save liquid
⅓ cup pitted oil cured olives or Kalamata olives
¼ cup organic golden raisins
⅓ cup toasted pine nuts
sea salt and freshly ground pepper

Garnish: grated Parmesan cheese

Steam the broccoli in a vegetable steamer or small amount of water in a covered saucepan for about 6–8 minutes. Transfer the broccoli to a large platter. Season with sea salt and a twist of pepper. Cover and set aside in a slightly warm oven.

In a large skillet, heat the oil. Add the onions and cook until browned. Add the wine, vinegar, tomato paste, oregano, pepper flakes, garlic and parsley and cook, stirring occasionally until the mixture is reduced and thick, 4–5 minutes. Add the plum tomatoes with the liquid and bring the sauce to a boil. Lower the heat to medium-low and simmer, uncovered, stirring occasionally about 8–10 minutes. Add the olives and simmer about 10 minutes more. Stir in the raisins.

Spoon the sauce over the room temperature broccoli and sprinkle with the toasted pine nuts. Pass the Parmesan.

Steamed Artichokes

My parents moved from Minnesota to the San Joaquin Valley in 1952 when I was six years old. When I started the first grade in Turlock, California, I would go to my friend's house so we could walk to school together. My first introduction to artichokes was observing my friend and her family eating them for breakfast. I have loved artichokes ever since. In California the large green globe artichoke comes from Monterey County, particularly the town of Castroville, the self proclaimed "Artichoke Capitol of the World."

Count on one artichoke per person . . . or a half if they are extra large.

First use a serrated knife to cut away the top of the artichoke about half way between the tip and the base. Cut the stem off of the bottom. I usually peel a few of the tough outer leaves off, too.

Bring water to a boil in a steamer and steam the artichokes until fork tender. Remove to a plate and place upside down to drain. To serve give each person their own artichoke on a salad plate. Serve with melted KerryGold butter and lemon wedges, Homemade Garlic Aioli or the Bagna Cauda.

To eat, peel each leaf off, dip the soft end of the leaf, where it attaches to the globe in your butter and then scrape the tender part off with your teeth. This can be a very messy, drippy, eating fest so if you are a fastidious eater, artichokes probably are not for you. After you have eaten the leaves, scoop out the choke part with a spoon and eat the creamy artichoke heart. Fantastic!

Chile Rellenos with Fresh Herb Salsa

Serves 6

The Chile Rellenos can be a main entrée or side dish. It is well worth the effort of blistering and peeling the chiles. If you don't like goat cheese, just use the jack or Manchego cheese. I served these as a first course for Christmas dinner in Santa Fe followed by roast turkey with the Mexican Mole. I cannot imagine a more special Christmas dinner. Serve the Chile Rellenos with a green salad with avocadoes, radishes, oranges and the Citrus Vinaigrette. The Grapefruit Salad would also be very nice. If you have leftover rellenos, cut them up and scramble them into your breakfast eggs. For a vegetarian dinner serve them with the Rice Verde.

12 anaheim or poblano chiles. I like the poblano as they are very meaty.
8 ounces goat cheese
2 cloves garlic, minced
2 tablespoons minced shallots
8 ounces jack cheese or Manchego
1 ripe tomato, diced
¼ cup cilantro leaves, chopped
½ cup basil leaves, thinly sliced
2 tablespoons heavy cream
1 egg
sea salt and fresh pepper
*cornmeal for coating
*sesame oil for frying

Prepare the chiles by blistering the skin on top of the fire (burner) if you have a gas stove or under the broiler in the oven. Keep turning the chiles so they blister evenly. Then place them in a brown paper bag to steam. When cool enough, peel the skins off, under running water or in a bowl of water. It's best to use gloves for this as you do not want to wipe your eyes and get chile seed oil in them.

Slice the chiles open and remove the seeds being careful not to tear the chiles. If you do happen to tear them you can press them back together when you put in the filling.

In a bowl, combine all the ingredients, except the egg and cream. Gently stuff the filling into the chiles and secure them with a toothpick. Set each chile aside as you do this.

In another bowl, beat the egg and cream together. While the sesame oil is heating in a large skillet, roll each chile, first in the egg and cream, and then in the cornmeal. Fry the chiles until they are golden brown all around. Place them in a shallow baking dish in a warm oven until ready to serve. Serve the Chile Rellenos with the Fresh Herb Salsa.

Fresh Herb Salsa:
>   2 shallots, finely minced
>   ½ cup Champagne vinegar
>   ¾ cup extra virgin olive oil
>   3 ripe tomatoes, peeled, seeded and chopped
>   1 tablespoon each fresh thyme, oregano and flat leaf parsley
>   sea salt and fresh pepper to taste

In a bowl whisk together the ingredients. Spoon the salsa over the Chile Rellenos.

Pesto Vegetables

Serves 6

Pesto vegetables are a meal in themselves. For this dish use whatever vegetables you fancy. I will just present an idea of what you can use here. Use the leftover pesto vegetables for your breakfast eggs.

> **1 pound asparagus or broccolini**
> **1 bunch kale**
> **1 onion, halved and sliced**
> **1 red, yellow, or orange bell pepper**
> **2 tablespoons cold pressed sesame oil**

Garnish: 1 cup organic cherry tomatoes, halved

In a large sauté pan cook the onion in the 2 tablespoons sesame oil until golden brown. Add the remaining vegetables (except the tomatoes) and cover. Cook the vegetables for a few minutes until just done. The vegetables should still be vibrant. Remove the lid and stir in approximately one cup of the pesto and mix well.

Turn the vegetables out onto a platter and surround with the cherry tomatoes. Grate some Parmesan cheese on the top for garnish. If you want to use a grain, serve the pesto vegetables with some cooked brown or wild rice or quinoa.

The Pesto:
The addition of the oregano in this pesto gives it an even more complex flavor.

> **6–8 large cloves garlic**
> **2 large bunches basil leaves (about 4 cups)**
> **1 small bunch oregano leaves, picked from stem (optional)**

½ cup pine nuts
juice of ½ lemon
⅔ cup grated Parmesan cheese
1 cup extra virgin olive oil
1 teaspoon sea salt & twist of pepper to taste

In a food processor, combine the garlic, basil, oregano, pine nuts, lemon juice, and the Parmesan. Turn on the processor and slowly pour in the olive oil; whirl until the mixture is very smooth, adding more oil if necessary. Season with the salt and pepper.

*Pack the leftover pesto, if there is any, in small jars topped with olive oil and refrigerate for up to a week, or just freeze.

What's for Dinner?

Wild-Caught Seafood

Grilled Skewered Prawn Kebabs with Chipotle, Cilantro, and Lime Dipping Sauce

Serves 4

The flavors of chipotle, cilantro and lime are straight from Mexico. The Rice Verde would also work with the kebabs.

The Sauce: *(to be prepared two hours in advance)*
¾ cup organic sour cream
1 teaspoon chipotle peppers, minced (chipotle peppers come in a small can in the Mexican section of the grocery store)
1 teaspoon of the chipotle adobo sauce
1 teaspoon cilantro leaves, finely chopped
½ teaspoon grated lime zest
1 tablespoon lime juice
1 teaspoon minced garlic
¼ teaspoon sea salt

In a bowl mix the ingredients. Cover and refrigerate for at least 2 hours.

3–4 jumbo prawns per person
2 red bell pepper cut into chunks
1 red onion, cut into chunks
8 large mushrooms
*sesame oil for brushing

Alternate the prawns, red bell pepper and mushrooms on long wooden skewers that have soaked in water for an hour. Brush the sewers with sesame oil and sprinkle with a little sea salt. Cook the kebabs on a hot grill or broil for 2–3 minutes per side. Serve the kebabs with small bowls of the dipping sauce for each person.

Sole with Browned Butter and Capers

Serves 2

Sole is always a favorite because of its delicacy. The browned butter sauce is perfection with the sole.

>   2-Pacific Rock Sole filets, about 4 ounces each (or Dover or Petrale sole)
>   sea salt & twist of freshly ground pepper
>   ¼ cup whipping cream
>   ¼ cup almond flour
>   2 tablespoons ghee or cold pressed sesame oil for frying fish

Sauce:
>   4 tablespoons KerryGold butter, for the sauce
>   juice of one lemon
>   2 teaspoons capers
>   2 tablespoons Italian flat leaf parsley, chopped
>   sea salt & twist of pepper

Place a large serving plate in the oven to warm at 200 degrees F.

Season the sole filets with salt & pepper and place them in a 9" glass pie pan. Cover with the milk and set aside.

Put the almond flour on a plate. Then remove the fillets from the cream, shake of any excess, and dredge both sides of the fillets in the flour.

In a skillet over medium high heat, warm the ghee. Cook the fillets on one side for about 2 minutes or until lightly browned, then carefully turn the fish and cook for 2 minutes more. Transfer the sole to the warm plate in the oven.

To make the sauce, in the same skillet, over medium high heat, add the unsalted butter and cook until it turns golden brown and has a nutty aroma. Remove the skillet from heat and whisk in the lemon juice, capers and parsley. Remove the sole from the warm oven and immediately pour the sauce over it. Serve hot.

A nice accompaniment to the sole would be steamed baby Brussels sprouts or spring asparagus spears.

Red Snapper Vera Cruz with Rice Verde

Serves 6

This dish just takes minutes to make. Serve the red snapper with a salad of greens, oranges, avocadoes and the Citrus Dressing. You will have a bright and festive dinner.

Six 4 ounce pieces of Hawaiian red snapper filet (1½ pounds)
2 tablespoons coconut or cold pressed sesame oil
1 large onion, thinly sliced
½ red bell pepper, thinly sliced
6 cloves garlic, minced
2 tablespoons jalapenos, seeded and chopped
4 organic plum tomatoes chopped
juice of one lime
½ cup green olives, pitted and chopped (Piccoline or Cerignola)
1 tablespoon fresh oregano
Celtic sea salt and fresh pepper to taste

Garnish: 3 limes cut into wedges, 2 tablespoons fresh parsley, chopped

Heat the oil in a large skillet over medium-high heat. Add the onion and cook, stirring occasionally, until golden, about 5–7 minutes. Add the red bell pepper, garlic and jalapeno and cook 1 minute more.

Add the tomatoes, ¾ cup of water and lime juice and cook until almost evaporated, 6–8 minutes. Stir in olives and oregano.

Season the snapper filets with the sea salt and pepper. Add the snapper to the pan with the sauce and reduce the heat to medium. Cover and cook until the fish is opaque, 5–7 minutes.

To serve place the snapper and green rice on the dinner plates. Sprinkle with the chopped parsley and garnish with the lime wedges.

Rice Verde

Serves 6

1 cup homemade vegetable or chicken broth
1¼ cup water
½ cup flat-leaf parsley (leaves only)
¼ cup mint leaves
2 teaspoons scallion, minced
¼ cup cilantro leaves
2 teaspoon fennel seeds, toasted slightly in a pan
¼ cup KerryGold butter
¾ cup fennel bulb, finely diced
¾ cup red onion, finely diced
¼ teaspoon red chile flakes
1½ cup brown basmati rice, pre-soaked for 6–8 hours, then rinsed
2 tablespoons KerryGold butter or ghee
sea salt and twist of pepper

In a medium pot bring the vegetable broth and water to a boil. Turn off the heat. In a blender place all the herbs. Add 1 cup of the hot liquid and puree the herbs. Slowly add the remaining liquid and puree for another 2 minutes, until the green broth is very smooth. Grind the toasted fennel seeds in the coffee grinder until almost a paste or pound them with a mortar and pestle if you have one.

In the same pot you used to heat the broth (rinse it out), heat it over high heat for 2 minutes. Add the butter, diced fennel and onion, chile flakes and ½ teaspoon sea salt. Lower the heat to medium and cook the mixture until the onions and the fennel are soft and translucent. Add the basmati rice, 1 teaspoon sea salt and a twist of pepper. Stir well to coat the rice with the vegetables. Add the herb broth and butter and bring to a boil. Then reduce the heat to low and simmer the rice for 15–20 minutes until tender.

Remove the rice from the heat and let stand covered for 5 minutes. Fluff the rice with a fork and serve.

Salmon with Haricots Verts, Eggs and Nicoise Olives

Serves 8

This is a simple summer supper that you can serve at room temperature. Make the Lemon-Oregano Vinaigrette in the salad section to dress the salmon and vegetables. As an alternative to salmon try Hawaiian Tombo tuna.

2 pounds Alaskan *wild-caught* **salmon filet, skin on**

Marinade:
In a bowl whisk together
> **2 tablespoons olive oil**
> **juice of one lemon**
> **1 teaspoon minced fresh thyme**
> **1 teaspoon lemon zest**
> **½ cup finely minced green onion**
> **¼ cup flat leaf parsley**
> **sea salt and fresh ground pepper**

> **8 hard boiled eggs, peeled and cut into wedges**
> **¾ pound steamed haricots verts, or another young and tender garden bean**
> **¼ cup pitted Nicoise olives**
> **¼ cup sliced radishes**
> **½ teaspoon sea salt and a twist of pepper**
> ***6 ounces of your favorite salad greens, arugula, red oak leaf, watercress, or mesclun**
> ***sliced avocado if you like**

Pre-heat the oven to 400 degrees F.

In a bowl whisk together the marinade. Place the salmon, skin side down, on a foiled sheet pan. Pour the marinade over the salmon and bake for 20 minutes or until *just done*. Salmon should be slightly pink and moist in the center. Remove the salmon from the oven.

In a pot with a steamer basket, steam the haricots verts until crisp and bright green.

To complete the dinner tear the salmon, with a fork, into 2" pieces.

Place some of the salad greens on each plate; arrange the hard boiled egg wedges, the radishes and haricots verts evenly around each plate. Then place the pieces of salmon artfully in the middle of the plate. Garnish the plates with the Nicoise olives, avocado slices and extra sprigs of fresh thyme and a light sprinkling of sea salt and pepper, if desired. Dress the entrée with the Lemon-Oregano Vinaigrette.

Thai Pineapple Red Curry with Coconut Brown Rice

Serves 4

The addition of fresh pineapple in this gorgeous red curry makes it absolutely mouth watering.

2½ cups unsweetened coconut milk
¼ cup (1 jar) Thai red curry paste
2 cups cooked shrimp or your choice of fish
juice and zest of one lime
1 cup fresh pineapple, cut in 1" chunks
½ cup chopped red bell pepper
2 tablespoons Nama Shoyu soy sauce or San-J *wheat-free* tamari
6 Thai chiles or jalapenos, seeded
¾ cup water
20 organic cherry tomatoes, left whole
10 Thai basil leaves

In a large saucepan, over medium heat, slightly reduce 1 cup of the coconut milk. This will take about 5 minutes. Whisk the red curry paste and continue to simmer about 5 more minutes.

Add the cooked chicken or seafood, stirring gently until the mixture is heated through, about 5 minutes.

Add the remaining coconut milk, lime juice, lime zest and water. Increase the heat and simmer until flavors meld, about 2 minutes.

Add the pineapple, red bell pepper, tamari, and chiles and continue to cook until the pineapple is tender, about 3–4 minutes. Just before serving toss in the tomatoes and the basil so they retain their flavor and color.

To serve place the curry in a large serving bowl with a ladle. Place the Coconut Brown Rice in another bowl and let everyone help themselves.

Coconut Brown Rice

Serves 6

This rice dish can be used as an accompaniment to many Asian recipes.

> **Two 1 inch pieces peeled fresh ginger**
> **2 cups brown jasmine rice, soaked in water 6–8 hours, then rinsed**
> **1½ cups coconut milk**
> **½ teaspoon sea salt**

Garnish: cilantro sprigs

With the back of a heavy bladed knife, smash the pieces of ginger until they flatten out and become stringy. Whack the ginger a couple of times.

Rinse the soaked rice thoroughly in a strainer under cold water. In a large saucepan with a lid place the rice, coconut milk, 1½ cups cold water and the sea salt. Add the ginger to the rice mixture and stir well, submerging the ginger before cooking.

Over high heat bring the rice to a boil; stirring constantly to prevent scorching. The mixture will begin to thicken. Let the rice boil for 15 seconds and then reduce the heat to medium low and simmer, covered until the liquid is completely absorbed. Remove the pan from the heat and let the rice sit for 10 minutes before serving.

To serve fluff the rice with a fork. Then transfer the rice to the serving bowl and garnish with sprigs of cilantro.

Salmon with Sour Cream-Dill Sauce

Serves 4

Salmon with sour cream and dill. Classic!

4 *wild-caught* salmon steaks or escallops, about 4 ounces per person
2 tablespoons extra virgin olive oil
Fresh cracked pepper
½ teaspoon Celtic salt

Sour Cream-Dill Sauce:
1 cup organic sour cream
3 tablespoons Champagne vinegar or white vinegar
3 tablespoons whole grain or Dijon mustard
2 tablespoons raw honey
6 tablespoons fresh dill, chopped
4 scallions very finely minced

6 cups very fresh watercress and arugula or other favorite greens

Mix the sour cream-dill sauce ingredients in a bowl and set aside.

Place the salmon on a plate and coat evenly with the sea salt and cracked pepper.

In a large bowl, toss the greens with a little olive oil making sure to coat the leaves well. Divide the greens onto four dinner plates.

In a heavy bottomed skillet heat the olive oil to medium-hot. Sear the salmon on each side for about 1 minute or a little longer. Salmon should remain nice and pink in the center.

Place the salmon on top of the greens. Drizzle some of the sauce over the salmon. Pass the remaining sauce.

Pan Seared Salmon with Avocado Slices and Lime Dressing

For 2

This is a very simple recipe that takes just minutes to make. The avocado complements the salmon perfectly. Serve with The Grapefruit Salad with Microgreens.

> 8 ounce piece *wild-caught* salmon escalope or steak (4 ounces per person)
> 2 tablespoons coconut oil
> ½ teaspoon Celtic salt, twist of pepper
> 1 small avocado, pit removed and sliced

Garnish: ½ cup sliced organic cherry tomatoes, generous sprigs of watercress

Lime dressing:
> 2 tablespoons extra virgin olive oil
> 3 tablespoons finely minced white onion
> 2 tablespoons chopped cilantro leaves
> 2–3 teaspoons fresh jalapeno peppers, seeded and finely diced
> 1 tablespoon fresh lime juice
> pinch sea salt

Whisk the ingredients in a bowl. Set aside.

In a heavy bottomed skillet on medium hot, heat the oil. Sear the salmon for 1–2 minutes on each side. Remove to the dinner plates. Serve topped with the avocado slices and the lime dressing.

Fish Tacos with Guacamole

Serves 6

I could eat fish tacos almost every day. Everyone loves them and they make a very economical and simple meal. The whole family can participate in the preparation. Yummy!

> 3 ounces per person of your favorite "cooked" fish (Pacific Cod, Rock Sole or shrimp)
> 12 Ezekiel sprouted corn tortillas
> sea salt & twist of pepper
> 3 tablespoons lime juice
> 2 cloves garlic, minced very fine
> 3 limes cut into wedges
> 5 large ripe tomatoes, peeled, seeded and chopped
> leaves from one bunch of cilantro
> 5 jalapeno chiles
> 2 poblano chiles, charred, peeled, seeded and chopped (optional)
> 1 large red onion halved through the root end and sliced very thin
> 1 pint organic sour cream (squeeze juice of one lime into the sour cream and mix)
> 2 cups of very thinly sliced red and green cabbage.
> 1 cup grated raw jack cheese or New Zealand *grass-fed* cheddar (Trader Joe's)

Salt and pepper your fish and then broil or grill to your taste. Cut into cubes and keep warm.

Warm the tortillas in a 300-degree oven wrapped in a slightly dampened towel and then aluminum foil. You can also fry the tortillas in a little sesame oil.

In separate colorful bowls place the fish cubes, tomatoes, red onion slices, cilantro leaves, chiles, shredded cabbage, guacamole, lime cream and lime wedges. Place the tortillas on a heated plate. Let everyone help themselves.

Guacamole:

> 2–3 large ripe avocadoes, peeled, seeded and roughly chopped
> 1 large vine ripened tomato, diced or ½ cup organic Mexican *sweet 100's* quartered
> 2 tablespoons red or yellow onion, minced
> 2 cloves garlic minced
> juice of ½ lime
> Sea salt and a twist of pepper to taste

In a bowl gently mix all the ingredients. I like to see all the ingredients but some like to mash everything together. Do your own thing.

Wild-Caught, Hickory Grilled Salmon with Pistachio Sauce and Grilled Vegetables

This is one of the best preparations for salmon I know, and I wanted to include it even though the recipe calls for brown sugar. This dish was on our *Best of Everything* catering menu for years and it was always a wedding favorite. Be sure to use *wild-caught* salmon. The piece should be thick. Note that the salmon must be coated with the salt and sugar mixture at least six hours before it is grilled. You can adjust the salt-sugar ratio depending on your own taste. Serve the salmon with the Middle East-inspired Pistachio Sauce and Grilled Vegetables (recipes below).

> **One side of** *wild-caught* **"Alaskan" salmon with the skin on (figure 3–4 ounces salmon per person)**
> **1 cup of organic brown sugar**
> **1 cup Celtic coarse grained sea salt or kosher salt**
> **1 cup hickory chips**

To prepare the salmon, combine the sugar and salt, rub generously over the salmon, then place the salmon on a sheet pan and refrigerate, preferably overnight.

Prepare the grill. Place your charcoal to one side of your grill and light. Place the hickory chips in water to soak. When the charcoal has burned down to a moderately slow heat, drain the hickory chips and add them to the coals. Place the salmon, skin side down, on an 'oiled' sheet of foil and then on the grill *opposite* the coals.

Cover the grill allowing enough air flow to maintain the heat. Grill indirectly until juices begin to flow and salmon exhibits some resistance to the touch. It should be mahogany in color (about 20–25 minutes).

Remove to platter and garnish with the Pistachio Sauce.

For the grilled vegetables, we would grill asparagus, onion wedges, eggplant, red bell peppers, cooked carrots, and pre-baked sweet potato slices. We would brush the veggies generously with olive oil and balsamic vinegar. Everyone loved these vegetables.

Grilled Vegetables:

It's best to grill your vegetables first and serve them warm or at room temperature.

> *pre-baked* sweet potatoes, sliced about 1 inch thick
> asparagus, tough ends removed
> red onion edges
> eggplant slices, 1 inch thick
> large mushrooms
> red bell pepper, large chunks
> carrots, trimmed and slightly pre-cooked
> vine ripened tomatoes cut in half

Marinade for vegetables:
> 1 cup cold pressed sesame oil
> 1 cup balsamic vinegar
> 3–4 shallots, finely minced
> 8 cloves garlic, finely minced
> Sea Salt and freshly ground pepper to taste

*In a bowl mix the marinade ingredients. Arrange the vegetables you are using on a large sheet pan and brush liberally with the marinade mixture before placing the vegetables on the grill. Keep brushing the vegetables with the marinade as they grill and also afterwards for an extra sheen.

Pistachio Sauce:

This rich sauce has a light green color, which goes beautifully with the color of the salmon.

> 1 cup shelled unsalted pistachios (you can rinse the pistachios of the salt)
> 1 cup freshly squeezed lemon juice
> 1 cup freshly squeezed orange juice
> 1 cup extra virgin olive oil
> 1 teaspoon sea salt and a twist of fresh pepper to taste

In a blender add the lemon juice and pistachios. Blend until the mixture is a smooth paste. With the blender still running, slowly add the orange juice and olive oil and process until the sauce thickens. The sauce should be "pourable" so you may need to add some more of the juices until the proper consistency is reached and the flavor is to your taste. Add the sea salt and pepper to taste and process the sauce again briefly to mix. Set sauce aside.

Hawaiian Red Snapper with Sweet and Sour Marinade

Serves 4

This dish is made the day before it is served to give the snapper time to marinate in the sauce. This is a perfect dish to serve company so you won't have to be in the kitchen cooking. It's nice for summer as it is served at room temperature.

> 1 pound Hawaiian red snapper filet (make sure the snapper is not the overfished variety)*

1 cup coconut oil
¼ cup brown rice flour
Celtic sea salt and freshly ground pepper
1 small red onion, cut in half and sliced thinly
¼ cup organic golden raisins
¼ cup pine nuts
1 tablespoon raw honey
¾ cups red wine vinegar
3 tablespoons chives or very finely diced scallion
1 celery stalk, 6 inches in length, sliced in paper thin "ribbons"
Juice of ½ lemon
2 tablespoons extra virgin olive oil

Season the snapper with the sea salt and pepper and then dredge in the flour on both sides.

In a heavy bottomed skillet heat ¾ cup of the coconut oil to medium hot and fry the fish on both sides until nicely browned about 4–6 minutes. Remove and drain on paper towels.

Wipe out the skillet with a paper towel and heat the remaining ¼ cup of oil over medium heat. Add the onion and cook until translucent, about 10 minutes. Add the raisins, pine nuts, honey and vinegar and bring to a boil. Cook for 5–6 minutes. Remove from heat and cool.

In a glass bowl layer the snapper pieces and the marinade ending with the marinade on top. Press plastic wrap on top of the seafood to make it airtight. Refrigerate for approximate 24 hours. Remove from the refrigerator 1 hour before serving.

To serve toss the celery slices in a small bowl with the lemon juice and 2 tablespoons of extra virgin olive oil. Place the snapper pieces in the center of 4 salad plates and spoon the red onion marinade evenly over the fish. Garnish each plate with a mound of the celery. Add a twist of pepper to each plate.

*Go to the Monterey Bay Aquarium Web site and read about all the fish varieties that you *can* eat.

Mardi Gras Crab Cakes with Creole Remoulade

Serves 4

I love crab cakes. The way I test a restaurant is by how good their crab cakes are. You need impeccably fresh crab. Dungeness crabs are caught all along the Pacific Coast from Alaska to Baja. The season is from November to June. Crab cakes make a nice brunch dish or a Sunday night supper. The fresh corn and red pepper give this recipe added color and a delicious taste.

> **1 pound fresh Dungeness crab meat. If your crab has been frozen, squeeze out the excess water before proceeding with the recipe.**
>
> **¼ cup Homemade Mayonnaise**
> **¼ cup fresh or frozen organic corn kernels**
> **1 bunch scallion, minced**
> **¼ cup red bell pepper, finely chopped**
> **1 egg, beaten**
> **1 teaspoon Worcestershire**
> **½ cup almond meal (you can use leftover almonds from making almond milk)***
> **dash of Tobasco Sauce**
> **pinch of sea salt & twist of pepper**
> ***sesame oil for frying**

Combine all of the ingredients in a bowl, except for the sesame oil. Mix until well blended but do not break the large pieces of the crab meat. Shape the mixture into 6 patties approximately 3 inches in diameter. If the mixture does not hold together add a little more of the almond meal.

Put some almond meal on a plate and coat the outside of the crab cakes on both sides. Then, in a large skillet heat the oil. Fry the crab cakes until golden on both sides. Transfer the crab cakes to a paper towel. Keep warm until ready to serve.

Serve the crab cakes with a very simple green salad. Pass the Remoulade.

*If you save the leftover almond meal make sure to dry it in a 150 oven first.

Creole Remoulade:

Remoulade is not the typical seafood sauce. It's very sophisticated and works perfectly with the crab cakes, a seafood salad (instead of that pink dressing) or as a dip for party shrimp.

> juice of one lemon
> peel of one organic lemon
> 1 egg
> ¼ cup Creole mustard
> ¼ cup creamed horseradish
> 1 teaspoon paprika
> 1 teaspoon sea salt
> 1 cup extra virgin olive oil
> ¼ cup Champagne vinegar
> 2 cloves garlic, minced
> 2 teaspoons Worcestershire
> 1 shallot, minced
> 4 tablespoons minced celery leaf

Using a paring knife, trim peel off lemon, thinly, so there is no white part. Juice the lemon. Set rind and juice aside.

In a bowl, whisk together egg, mustard, horseradish, sea salt and paprika into a small bowl. Gradually whisk in oil until emulsified.

Whisk in vinegar, lemon juice, garlic, parsley, shallot, celery leaf, and Worcestershire. Add the bay leaf and the lemon rind and stir.

Place the mixture in a jar and refrigerate for 6 hours or overnight, then remove the bay leaf and rind.

Wild Striped Bass with Tangerines and Forbidden Rice

Serves 4

The combination of the bass with the tangerines and black rice is unusually eye appealing.

> 1 pound *wild-caught* striped bass filets (4 ounces per person)
> 2 tangerines
> 1 cup fresh tangerine juice
> zest of 2 tangerines
> 2 teaspoons fresh thyme leaves
> 1½ tablespoons flat leaf parsley, chopped
> 2 tablespoons cold pressed sesame oil
> 1 tablespoon raw honey
> 4 tablespoons KerryGold butter
> sea salt and a twist of black pepper

In a bowl combine the zest, thyme and parsley. Coat the fish fillets with this mixture and refrigerate, covered for 4–5 hours. Bring the fish to room temperature about 20 minutes before cooking. Season with a little sea salt and the freshly ground black pepper.

With a very sharp knife remove the peeling from the tangerine, pith and all. Then slice between the membranes to release each individual segment. Place segments in a bowl.

In a large sauté pan over medium high heat, add the oil, swirling it in the pan. Sauté the fish, skin side down, for 3–4 minutes until the skin is crisp and light brown. Turn the fish and cook a few minutes more until is just done. Be careful not to overcook the fish.

Wipe the pan out and return it to the medium-high heat. Add the tangerine juice and honey and bring to a boil. Reduce the juice by half and then whisk in the butter. Remove from heat and add the tangerine segments.

To serve place the Forbidden Rice in the middle of each dinner plate. Place a piece of bass on top of the rice and spoon the sauce and the tangerine segments on top. Garnish with a sprig of thyme.

Forbidden Rice

Forbidden rice is a very unusual, rare variety of rice. It has a wonderful nutty flavor and pairs beautifully with fish, meats, or vegetables. It would be spectacular to use in a stir-fry or salad.

> **1 cup Lotus Foods Forbidden Rice (black rice). Soak overnight and rinse well before cooking.**
> **1 tablespoon cold pressed sesame oil**
> **½ cup diced onion**
> **¼ teaspoon red chile flakes**
> **1 teaspoon thyme leaves**
> **pinch teaspoon sea salt**
> **¼ cup white wine**
> **2 cups water**
> **2 tablespoons KerryGold butter or ghee**
> **twist of pepper**

In a large sauté pan heat the oil. Add the onion, chile flakes and thyme. Cook while stirring until the onion gets soft and translucent. Add the rice, coating it with the onion mixture. Keep stirring while the rice toasts. Add the white wine and cook for 2 minutes. Add 2 cups water and pinch sea salt and bring to a boil. Cover and cook for 30 minutes or until tender (slightly al dente). Stir in the butter and add the twist of pepper.

Cacciucco

Serves 8 lavishly

I had the best Tuscan seafood stew of my life in a restaurant in Florence, Italy with my friend Sharon Dellamonica. After I ate the dish once, I went back to the restaurant and ate it again. The fish and shellfish were impeccably fresh. This is a special dish to be shared with friends and a good wine.

⅓ cup extra virgin olive oil
6 cloves garlic, chopped
1 tablespoon Italian parsley, chopped
1 tablespoon fresh sage leaves, chopped
½ teaspoon red pepper flakes
½ pound calamari cleaned and cut into 1" pieces
1 tablespoon organic tomato paste*
1 cup Pinot Noir or Sauvignon Blanc
One 14 ounce can organic plum tomatoes and juice (chop the tomatoes)
2 cups shellfish stock or vegetable broth
4 tablespoons KerryGold butter
1 pound red snapper cut into 2" pieces
1 pound large shrimp with heads & shells on
1 pound mussels*
sea salt and freshly ground pepper

In a large soup pot over medium heat add ¼ cup of the extra virgin olive oil, then the garlic, parsley, sage and red pepper flakes. Cook for about one minute. Add the calamari, and cook until opaque, stirring occasionally, about 4–5 minutes. Add tomato paste and mix well, 1 minute.

Add the wine and cook, stirring often, until the liquid has evaporated, about 20 minutes.

Add the tomatoes and juice to the calamari and season with salt and pepper to taste. Squid should be tender. Stir in the fish stock, butter, the snapper and then the shrimp and place the mussels evenly over the top. Cook, covered, without stirring, until the snapper is just cooked and the mussels have opened, about 10 minutes. Discard any unopened mussels.

To serve the stew, ladle into large white bowls with wide rims. Drizzle the top of the stew with a little more olive oil.

*When you have leftover tomato paste, put it in a small plastic container or glass jar and freeze it for next time.

*mussels are farm raised. Read about them on Blue Ocean Institute Web site *www.blueocean.org/programs/seafood-search.*

Grass-Fed Meats

Broiled Marinated Flank Steak

Serves 8

Steak never fails to please and marinated flank steak is full of flavor. The steak needs to marinate overnight for best results. Serve with a simple salad, or sliced garden tomatoes and the Grilled Asparagus. This is a very easy dinner to prepare.

2 pounds *grass-fed* **beef flank steak**

The Marinade:
> **1 bunch cilantro, coarsely chopped, about 1½ cups**
> **4–5 tablespoons of** *microplaned* **ginger**
> **1 cup Nama Shoyu soy sauce or San-J** *wheat-free* **tamari**
> **1 cup dry sherry**
> **1 tablespoon raw honey**
> **6 cloves garlic, minced**
> **2 tablespoons red pepper flakes**

In the food processor place the chopped cilantro, the grated ginger, and the remaining marinade ingredients. Blend until the mixture is pureed.

Trim the flank steak of excess fat. Place the steak in two 9 x 13 inch rectangular glass pans. Pour the marinade evenly over the steak. Cover and refrigerate overnight, turning occasionally.

To prepare for cooking, remove the flank steak from the refrigerator and bring to room temperature, about 1 hour.

Turn the oven on to broil. Remove the steak from the marinade and place on the broiling pan.

Broil the steak for 2–3 minutes on each side, or until rare. Slice thinly *against* the grain of the meat.

Long Meadow Ranch Grass-Fed Meatloaf

Serves 6

Long Meadow Ranch is a 650-acre working ranch nestled in the Mayacamas Mountains above the Napa Valley. My daughter and her husband lived at the ranch for a couple of years and helped manage the herd of Scottish Highland cows. My grandson Michael's job was feeding the chickens. In addition to raising beef, Long Meadow Ranch produces award-winning wines and hand crafted extra virgin olive oil, eggs, and heirloom fruits and vegetables. They sell their fine products every week at the St. Helena farmer's market. Here is their delicious recipe for Laddie's Meat Loaf. *www.longmeadowranch.com*

1½ pounds of LMR grass-fed Highland ground beef
½ cup milk
1 slightly beaten egg
1½ teaspoons Worcestershire Sauce
1 teaspoon salt
½ teaspoon dry mustard
Several "grinds" of pepper
1½ cups soft breadcrumbs (for a gluten-free version use 1 cup of cooked brown rice)
1 cup sliced mushrooms
½ onion, chopped
2–3 hardboiled eggs (optional), peeled
4 tablespoons catsup
2 tablespoons molasses

Preheat oven to 350 degrees.

In a mixing bowl combine milk, lightly beaten egg, Worcestershire sauce, seasonings and breadcrumbs. Let stand for about 5 minutes. Stir in ground beef, mushrooms and onion; mix lightly but thoroughly. Shape meat mixture into loaf while placing eggs center.

Place the meatloaf in 13" x 9" x 2" baking dish. Bake for 1 hour.

In a bowl combine catsup and molasses; brush on meatloaf after 1 hour and return to the oven for approximately 10 minutes. Makes a tasty glaze.

To serve, slice across the loaf revealing a cross section of eggs and place on a plate. Garnish with parsley.

Greek Lamb Kebabs with Tzatziki

Serves 8

Tzatziki is a traditional yogurt cucumber sauce in Greece. Serve the succulent lamb kebabs with the Spinach and Feta Salad as an accompaniment. For dessert roast some figs, sprinkle with a few drops of balsamic vinegar and drizzle with a little honey. Slices of late summer melon would also be perfect.

> 2 pounds *grass-fed* leg of lamb cut into 2" cubes (3–4 ounces per person)
> 1 small red onion cut into chunks to fit on skewers
> 2 red bell pepper cut into 1 inch chunks

Garnish:
> 1 cup flat-leaf parsley leaves, chopped
> 4 scallions, thinly sliced on the diagonal

Marinade:
> 2 cups hearty red wine
> 2 teaspoons dried oregano
> 1 tablespoon ground cumin
> 2 teaspoons dried thyme
> 1 teaspoon cinnamon
> 6 cloves of garlic smashed
> 2 teaspoons sea salt and freshly ground pepper to taste

*In a bowl whisk together the marinade. Add the cubed lamb and toss well. Cover the bowl with plastic wrap and marinate the meat at room temperature for 2 hours or in the refrigerator overnight.

Tzatziki:

¾ cup Mediterranean cucumbers, finely diced (these cucumbers are very small and sweet)

1 cup thick Greek Yogurt

1 scant teaspoon minced garlic

2 teaspoons fresh lemon juice

2 tablespoons fresh mint leaves, chopped

4 tablespoons extra virgin olive oil

pinch of sea salt and a twist of pepper

*In a bowl mix all the ingredients and season with the salt. Cover and refrigerate until ready to use. You can make the tzatziki a day in advance.

Turn the oven on to broil and arrange the rack about 7–8 inches from the element.

Remove the lamb from the marinade (reserve the marinade). Thread the lamb cubes (4 ounces each) on metal skewers, alternating with chunks of red onion and red bell pepper. Season the lamb with a sprinkle of sea salt and a twist of fresh pepper.

Pour the marinade into a small saucepan and bring to a boil, then turn the sauce down to a simmer. Broil the kebabs, generously basting with the marinade as they cook. Turn the kebabs until they are evenly brown on all sides and are still slightly pink in the middle, about 15–20 minutes.

To serve, plate the kebabs and garnish with the scallions and parsley. Pass the tzatziki.

Grilled Flank Steak with Salsa Verde

Serves 4

This is a family dinner that will please everyone. The steak would be great with the Grilled Vegetables or just simple sautéed vegetables of your choice.

1 pound *grass-fed* **flank steak, trimmed of excess fat**

Marinade:
> **¾ cup extra virgin olive oil**
> **4 cloves garlic, minced**
> **4 tablespoons minced fresh rosemary**
> **4 tablespoons minced fresh thyme**
> **4 tablespoons chopped fresh Italian parsley**

To prepare the steak mix the marinade ingredients in a small bowl and then pour the mixture into a 9 x 13 inch rectangular glass pan. Place the steak in the pan and coat both sides with the marinade. Cover with plastic wrap and place in the refrigerator for 4 hours minimum, turning the steak several times.

Salsa Verde:
Makes 1½ cups
> **1 cup extra virgin olive oil**
> **1 cup Italian flat leaf parsley, leaves only**
> **1 cup of fresh mint, leaves only**
> **1 bunch of very fresh basil leaves**
> **½ cup capers, rinsed and drained**

1 tablespoon Dijon mustard

2–3 tablespoons anchovy paste or 2 salt packed anchovy filets rinsed and drained

1 teaspoon Celtic sea salt

1 packet stevia

2 tablespoons freshly ground pepper

1 tablespoon red chile flakes

2 cloves garlic, minced

For the Salsa Verde place all the ingredients except the olive oil in the food processor. Turn the machine on and pulse until everything is a coarse paste. With the motor running slowly drizzle in the olive oil until the desired smoothness. The Salsa Verde will keep for a week in the refrigerator "capped" with a little olive oil. Great for breakfast eggs.

Prepare the grill and heat to medium-hot. Wipe the excess marinade off the steak with a paper towel and place on the grill. Cook the meat for 3–4 minutes on one side and turn and cook for another 3 minutes or until desired doneness. Grass Fed meat is best rare to medium rare.

Remove the steak from the grill when done and let rest for 3–5 minutes. Slice and serve. Pass the Salsa Verde.

Grilled Rib Eye Steak with Dry Steak Rub

Serves 4

You will want to marinate this steak for 24 hours prior to cooking. The Rib Eye is perfect with the Grilled Vegetables and The Savory Green Salad. What a nice dinner!

> **1 pound** *grass-fed* **boneless ribeye steak, about 4 ounces per person, 2 inches thick**

Dry Steak Rub:
  - 3 tablespoons ground cumin
  - 2 tablespoons freshly ground pepper
  - 2 tablespoons Chimayo chile powder
  - 1 tablespoon garlic powder
  - 1 tablespoon fennel seed
  - 1 tablespoon ground coriander
  - 1 tablespoon ground nutmeg
  - 1 tablespoon Celtic sea salt
  - 1 packet stevia

In a small bowl combine the ingredients and mix well. Rub a portion of the mixture liberally over the steak on both sides. Reserve the remaining rub for another use. You can make more of the rub and then have it on hand for next time. After coating the steak with the rub wrap it in plastic and refrigerate for 24 hours.

Olive and Balsamic Vinegar Sauce:
    ¼ **cup extra virgin olive oil**
    2–3 **tablespoons good quality balsamic vinegar**

Whisk the oil and vinegar together.

To cook the steak, preheat the grill or broiler. Remove the ribeye from the refrigerator and wipe off excess rub with a paper towel. Grill or broil the meat for about 20 minutes or until the desired doneness. The steak is best rare or medium rare. Turn the steak as it cooks every 6 minutes or so. Remove the steak from the grill and let it rest for about 5 minutes before slicing.

  To plate the steak have your grilled vegetables divided onto 4 dinner plates. Arrange the steak slices on top of the grilled vegetables and then spoon the sauce over everything. Pass the salad.

Short Ribs Braised in Zinfandel

Serves 8

For a rich and satisfying dinner, serve these succulent ribs with the Sautéed Greens and the Roasted Winter Vegetables. Marinate the ribs overnight. After that they are very simple to prepare.

8 grass-fed beef short ribs

1 cup chopped onions
½ cup leeks chopped and rinsed of any grit
1 Granny Smith apple, chopped
6 cloves garlic
2 jalapeno peppers
4 tablespoons cold pressed sesame oil
4 cups Zinfandel
5 tablespoons extra virgin olive oil
4 sprigs fresh thyme
4 fresh sage leaves
1 teaspoon coriander seeds wrapped in cheesecloth
4 cups homemade chicken or vegetable stock

In a large sauté pan heat the oil and caramelize the onions, leeks, apple, garlic and jalapenos, 7–10 minutes. Add the Zinfandel and bring to a simmer. Remove from heat and cool. Transfer the mixture to a large rectangular glass baking dish and place the short ribs in the marinade. Add 3 tablespoons of the olive oil, the thyme sprigs, sage leaves and the coriander seeds wrapped in the cheesecloth. Season the ribs with sea salt and freshly ground pepper. Coat the ribs very well with the marinade mixture, cover with plastic wrap and refrigerate for 24 hours.

Heat oven to 350 degrees.

In a heavy bottomed skillet sear the short ribs in 2 tablespoons of peanut oil for 2–3 minutes on each side, or until nicely browned. Place the ribs in a roasting pan and cover with the chicken stock and the marinade. Cover with foil and braise for 3–4 hours until the meat is fork tender. Remove short ribs from oven, and set aside. Strain the braising juices into a saucepan and reduce sauce to 1½ cups.

Before serving place the ribs in a baking dish in a 350 degree oven to 5–10 minutes to reheat.

To plate, place the sautéed greens in the center of the dinner plates. Place one short rib on top of the greens. Surround the ribs with some of the roasted vegetables and spoon the reduced sauce over the ribs.

Blue Cheese Burger on a Butter Lettuce "Bun"

For 2

This delicious burger has no bun. You will never miss it. Serve the burger with the homemade Grilled Tomato Ketsup.

    8 ounces *grass-fed* ground beef or ground turkey
    1 medium yellow onion thinly sliced
    2 tablespoons peanut oil
    2 teaspoons organic sour cream
    1 tablespoon Grilled Tomato Ketsup or barbecue sauce
    1½ teaspoons Worcestershire sauce
    Celtic sea salt and twist of pepper

    4 butter lettuce leaves
    4 ounces Pt. Reyes Blue, Maytag Blue, or another rich blue cheese of your choice

Garnish: Thick sliced garden tomatoes, avocado slices and sweet red onion slices. More Grilled Tomato Ketsup.

In a heavy bottomed skillet slowly caramelize the onions until brown and creamy.

In a bowl combine the ground beef, caramelized onions, sour cream, Ketsup and Worcestershire sauce. Season with a little sea salt and a couple twists of pepper and mix well. Divide the mixture into two balls and then form into patties about ¾ inch thick.

In a heavy bottomed skillet heat the oil over medium-high heat and brown the meat for about 1–2 minutes on each side. Rare is good.

Place one large butter lettuce leaf in the center of the dinner plate. Place the hamburger in the center of the plate and top with the blue cheese and your chosen garnishes. Add another twist of pepper if desired and then place the last butter lettuce leaf on top.

Lamb Chops with Cumin Yogurt and Oregano Pesto

Serves 4

This Middle Eastern flavored lamb is succulent and delicious. Serve with a spinach salad with Persian cucumbers, Kalamata olives and thick slices of ripe tomatoes.

3 lamb rib chops per person. Try the racks of New Zealand *grass-fed lamb* **at Trader Joe's (freezer section) and cut them into chops.**

Marinade:
¼ cup fresh mint leaves finely chopped
2 tablespoons extra virgin olive oil
Zest of 1 lemon
1 teaspoon Celtic sea salt and a twist of pepper

In the bowl of the food processor, blend the marinade ingredients until a rough paste is formed. Rub the marinade over the surface of all the lamb chops and set aside.

Cumin Yogurt:
1 cup thick Greek yogurt
1 tablespoon toasted ground cumin. Toast briefly in small sauté pan.
1 tablespoon extra virgin olive oil
1 tablespoon lemon juice
pinch of sea salt and twist of pepper

Mix ingredients in a small bowl. Set aside.

Oregano Pesto:

> 2 cups fresh oregano leaves, preferably from the garden (no stems)
> ¼ cup pine nuts
> 2 cloves garlic
> 1 teaspoon lemon juice
> ¼–⅓ cup extra virgin olive oil
> pinch sea salt and twist of pepper

Place the ingredients, except for the olive oil, in the food processor. With the motor running, slowly add the olive oil until well blended and smooth.

Garnish: Zest of 2 lemons (with a lemon zester-long strips). Sprigs of fresh mint.

To cook pre-heat the grill or broiler. Cook the chops rare to medium rare, 4–5 minutes on each side.

To serve place the lamb chops on each plate and arrange the spinach salad on the side. Drizzle the yogurt sauce around the mound of chops and then drizzle the pesto around as well. Garnish the lamb chops with the lemon zest and sprigs of fresh mint.

Pastured Poultry

Chicken "Scallopini" with Lemon-Caper Sauce

Serves 6

Three 8 ounce boneless and skinless *pastured* or organic free-range chicken breasts, (cut in half and pounded fairly flat)
1 cup brown rice flour
1 cup grated Parmesan cheese
6 tablespoons chopped parsley leaves
1 tablespoon chopped fresh rosemary
2 large eggs, beaten
6 tablespoons sesame oil
splash of white wine
6 tablespoons KerryGold butter
2 cloves of garlic, minced
juice of one lemon
2 tablespoons capers, rinsed
Sea salt and a twist of pepper

In a glass pie pan, mix the flour, Parmesan, parsley and rosemary. Add the beaten eggs to another glass pie pan.

Dredge the chicken breasts first in the beaten eggs and then flour-Parmesan mix. Salt and pepper the breasts and set aside.

In a large sauté pan over medium high, heat the oil. Sauté each breast until golden brown on each side. Add a little more oil to the pan if necessary. Hold the cooked breasts in a warm oven until ready to serve. In the same pan that you sautéed the chicken breasts, with the heat on medium high, deglaze the pan with the splash of white wine. Add 3–4 tablespoons of the butter, garlic, the lemon juice and the capers and whisk to incorporate. You may add a little more butter if necessary. Immediately remove sauce from heat and set aside.

Take the chicken breasts out of the oven and slice each breast on the diagonal (optional step). Arrange the chicken on the dinner plates with the haricots verts and spoon some of the sauce over the top.

Sunday Roast Chicken with Herb Compound Butter and Roasted Vegetables

Serves 6

We used to have roast chicken every Sunday when I was growing up. Roast chicken is family comfort food. With this dish you can put everything in the roasting pan and relax while dinner cooks. What could be more comforting than that? A nice accompaniment would be the Savory Green Salad.

One 4 pound *pastured* (if available) or organic free-range chicken. Rinse and pat dry.
1 cube KerryGold or other pastured butter, softened to room temperature
1 teaspoon minced garlic
4 tablespoons minced fresh rosemary, chopped parsley, and oregano
1 teaspoon Celtic sea salt
½ teaspoon freshly ground pepper
2 tablespoons lemon juice
zest of one lemon
½ cup red or white wine
1 tablespoon brown rice flour
additional sea salt and freshly ground pepper

The Vegetables:
1 tablespoon fennel seeds
12 cloves garlic, crushed
3 medium turnips, washed and cut into 1 inch pieces
3 medium parsnips, washed and cut into 1 inch pieces
sea salt & freshly ground pepper

1 large yellow onion, peeled of outside skin and cut into 6 wedges
few sprigs of fresh thyme
¾ pound shitake mushrooms (tough part of stem trimmed) or small button mushrooms left whole
1 fennel bulb sliced thin
¾ pound Brussels sprouts (optional)
12 large sage leaves
juice of one lemon

Preheat the oven to 400 degrees. In a small bowl mix the butter, garlic, herbs, salt, pepper, lemon juice and zest.

Carefully slide your hand in between the skin on the breast of the chicken and the flesh to make a pocket. Spread one half of the compound butter liberally over the inside pocket of the chicken, then rub the remaining herb butter over the entire outside of the chicken. Sprinkle the outside of the chicken with a little more sea salt and pepper. Tie the legs together with kitchen string and place the chicken on a roasting rack in a large roasting pan. Arrange turnips, onion, parsnips, and fennel around the chicken.

Roast the chicken for 30 minutes and then pour the wine over the top. *Lower the oven temperature to 350.*

In a large bowl mix the fennel seeds, thyme sprigs, garlic, Brussels sprouts, mushrooms, onions, and sage leaves with a little olive oil. Sprinkle with sea salt and pepper and add to the roasting pan. Continue roasting another 1 to 1½ hours, basting the chicken and vegetables every 20 minutes or so.

To test for doneness stick the tip of a sharp knife between where the leg attaches to the body of the chicken to make sure the juice is clear and not bloody. Transfer the chicken and the vegetables to a platter on top of the stove and cover with foil to keep warm.

While the chicken is resting pour the pan juices into a saucepan and bring to a simmer. Whisk in the tablespoon of flour and cook for 10 minutes. Thin the sauce with water or a little additional wine. Taste for seasonings.

To serve squeeze the lemon juice over the chicken and serve with the vegetables. Pass the sauce.

Roasted Duck Breasts with Wild Rice and Pear Salad

8 Servings

Duck is rarely served these days but it is rich and full of flavor. Serve duck during the holidays as an alternative to turkey and ham. Steamed Brussels sprouts would be the vegetable of my choice with this festive meal. Reserve the duck fat from the roasting pan to use as a delicious fat for cooking breakfast eggs.

  4 large duck breasts
  ½ teaspoon fennel seeds
  ¼ teaspoon ground coriander
  ½ teaspoon freshly ground pepper
  2 teaspoons Celtic sea salt
  zest of one organic orange
  2 teaspoons fresh thyme leaves
  ¼ cup fresh orange juice
  ¼ cup good quality port

Grind the fennel in the spice grinder and combine with the coriander, black pepper, salt, orange zest and thyme leaves. In a small bowl mix the port and the orange juice. With the tip of a very sharp knife score the fat on the duck breasts in a crisscross pattern. Rub the duck breasts with a teaspoon of the port-orange mixture and then sprinkle with some of the spice mixture. Reserve the remaining port/orange juice mixture for the sauce. Set the duck breasts aside on a plate while making the rice.

For the Sauce:
  2 tablespoons KerryGold butter
  2 tablespoons minced shallots
  ½ cup homemade chicken stock

6 sprigs of fresh thyme
zest of 2 oranges
1 cinnamon stick
⅛ teaspoon good quality paprika (optional)
the remaining port/orange juice mixture
pinch sea salt & twist of pepper

Preheat the oven to 400 degrees.

In a medium saucepan bring the butter, shallots, chicken stock, thyme, orange zest, cinnamon stick, paprika, the remaining port and orange juice to a boil. Reduce the mixture to ½ or until it reaches the consistency of a light syrup. Season with the salt and pepper. Remove from heat while duck breasts cook.

To cook the duck breasts bring a large cast iron skillet to medium-high heat. Place the duck breasts in the pan, skin side down and cook until the skin is a deep golden brown and the duck fat is rendered into the pan. Turn the breasts over and put the skillet in the oven and continue to cook the breasts until the internal temperature reaches 135 with an instant read thermometer, 4–8 minutes depending on the size of the duck breasts. I like my duck medium rare. When the duck breasts are done immediately transfer to a plate to rest. Reheat the sauce.

With a sharp knife, slice the duck breast at an angle to get long slices. Fan the slices onto the dinner plates with the wild rice salad and spoon the sauce over the top.

Wild Rice Salad:
1¼ pounds wild rice, soaked in water overnight and rinsed, then cooked according to package directions
2 large ripe organic pears, halved lengthwise, seeds removed, and sliced about ¼ inch thick
8 ounces Arugula, meslcun or watercress
½ cup toasted hazelnuts, walnuts, or pecans
½ cup fresh mint, finely chopped
2 scallions, thinly sliced on the diagonal

Dressing:

> ¾ cup extra virgin olive oil
> ¾ cup fresh organic orange juice
> 2 tablespoons *microplaned* orange zest
> 3 tablespoons maple syrup
> 1 tablespoon Dijon mustard
> ¼ teaspoon Celtic salt and twist of fresh pepper

In a large bowl whisk together the olive oil, orange juice, orange zest, maple syrup, sea salt, and twist of pepper. Add the cooked rice, hazelnuts, mint, and scallions. Toss well to mix dressing.

Baked Cilantro Chicken with Tomato-Avocado Salsa

Serves 6

These are the flavors I love, fresh and vibrant. Serve the chicken with the Caesar Salad.

> Three 8 ounce *free-range,* organic chicken breasts, bone and skin removed, cut in half
> ¼ cup extra virgin olive oil
> ¼ cup lime juice
> ¾ tablespoon ground cumin
> ½ cup cilantro, chopped
> pinch of sea salt and twist of black pepper

In a large bowl, whisk together all the ingredients. Place the chicken breasts in a 9 x 13 inch glass baking dish and pour the marinade over and coat well. Let stand for 30 minutes, turning occasionally.

Preheat oven to 350 degrees F.

Discard marinade and bake the chicken breasts for 20 minutes, until no longer pink in center. Remove the chicken breasts from the oven and plate the breasts. Spoon the salsa on top of the breasts.

* The chicken breasts may also be grilled.

Tomato-Avocado Salsa:
Prepare salsa at least 1 hour prior to serving to give time to chill.

> 2 baskets "Sweet 100's" organic Mexican cherry tomatoes cut in half
> 2 jalapeno chiles, seeded and thinly sliced
> ½ cup scallions, thinly sliced
> ½ cup Champagne vinegar
> 3 tablespoons raw honey
> 4 tablespoons microplaned ginger
> 2 tablespoons garlic, minced
> 2 teaspoons ground cumin
> 2 teaspoons yellow mustard seeds
> 1 teaspoon red chile flakes
> ½ cup extra cold pressed sesame oil
> 2 large avocadoes cut into chunks
> 1 teaspoon sea salt and a twist of fresh pepper

In a bowl combine the tomatoes, chiles, and green onions. In another bowl combine the ginger, garlic, and the dry spices.

In a saucepan over medium heat bring the vinegar and honey to a boil, for one minute. Remove from heat and add. Set aside.

In another saucepan heat the oil over medium heat; add the dry spice mixture and cook for 1 minute. Then add the seasoned vinegar, the salt and pepper and pour over the tomato mixture. Let the salsa chill at least 1 hour and up to four hours before serving. Just before serving add the avocados.

Pad Thai

Serves 8 generously

This is an extravagant and colorful dinner with complex Thai flavors. If you learn to make this recipe you can have your Thai dinner at home each week. I have taken the noodles out of this recipe. If you would rather have buckwheat noodles with this dish, just cook the noodles according to the package directions. Mix some of the dressing with the noodles before plating the Pad Thai.

*Prepare Pad Thai Sauce first. Recipe follows.

> ½ savoy cabbage, core removed and thinly sliced
> 3 cups cooked fish or shrimp, shells removed (you could also use leftover shredded chicken or beef)
> 4 tablespoons cold pressed sesame oil
> 4 tablespoons dried shrimp
> ½ teaspoon red chile flakes
> ¼ cup carrots, cut into matchsticks
> ¼ cup red bell pepper, thinly sliced
> 3 teaspoons minced garlic
> 1 tablespoon Nama Shoyu or San-J wheat-free tamari
> 6–8 green onions, thinly sliced on the diagonal
> one pound of bean sprouts
> juice of two limes
> ¾ cup roasted macadamia nuts, chopped fine in food processor

Garnish: sprigs of cilantro, 8 lime wedges, remaining bean sprouts

First shred the cabbage thinly and place it in large bowl. Set side.

In a wok or a large frying pan, heat the sesame oil. When the oil is hot, add the dried shrimp and the chile flakes. Stir for several seconds and then add the, carrots and red bell pepper and garlic in that order. Stir fry until the garlic is light brown.

Quickly add the cooked fish or shrimp, tamari, lime juice, and Phat Thai Sauce*. And mix well. Then add the green onions and ⅓ of the bean sprouts. Stir in ¼ cup of the roasted chopped macadamia nuts. Keep stirring until heated throughout.

To serve, place the shredded cabbage on a large platter and then pour the remaining ingredients over the top.

Garnish with the remaining bean sprouts, macadamia nuts, cilantro springs and lime wedges. Serve warm.

*If using the buckwheat noodles, place them on top of the cabbage and then add the warm seafood and vegetable mixture.

*Pad Thai Sauce
    3 ounces preserved tamarind paste
    10 tablespoons hot water
    4 teaspoons sea salt
    1 tablespoon of raw honey (to taste)
    ¾ cup white vinegar
    ¾ to 1 cup water

In a small bowl soak the tamarind paste in the hot water for 30 minutes, until soft. Place the pulp and water in the food processor and pulse to a paste. Press the paste through a sieve into a medium saucepan. Add the salt, sugar, vinegar and ¾–1 cup water. Boil over high heat for about 10 minutes, stirring constantly. Remove from heat and cool.

Makes 2¼ cups. You can make the sauce the day before.

Macadamia Chicken with Tangerine-Ginger Sauce

Serves 6

The macadamia nuts make this a very rich dish. Serve with a light refreshing salad or very simple steamed vegetables.

> **Three 8 ounce boned and skinned** *pastured or free-range*, **organic chicken breasts, cut in half**
> **1 cup coconut flour**
> **1 can coconut milk**
> **1 cup finely ground macadamia nuts (ground in food processor)**
> **Celtic sea salt and freshly ground pepper**
> **2 tablespoons KerryGold butter**
> **2 tablespoons coconut oil**
> **1 cup finely minced yellow onion**
> **2 tablespoons** *microplaned* **ginger**
> **2 tablespoons minced garlic**
> **1 cup homemade chicken or vegetable broth**
> **½ cup dry white wine**
> **½ cup fresh tangerine juice**

Preheat oven to 375 degrees F.

Put flour and 1 cup of the coconut milk in separate glass pie pans. Place the finely ground macadamia nuts on a dinner plate. Reserve the remaining coconut milk for the sauce.

Rinse the chicken breasts and pat dry. Season with the sea salt and pepper.

In a large sauté pan over medium high heat warm the coconut oil and butter together. Dredge the chicken breasts first in the flour, shaking off the excess, then the coconut milk and then press them into the macadamia nuts on both sides.

Sauté the breasts on both sides until golden brown, turning carefully so you won't break the nut coating. Transfer the chicken breasts to a 9 x 13 inch glass baking dish and bake until no longer pink in the middle, about 15–20 minutes.

Wipe out the sauté pan with a paper towel and add 1 more tablespoon of butter and 1 more tablespoon of coconut oil to the pan. Over medium heat cook the onions, garlic and ginger, stirring often until the onions begin to brown, about 5 minutes. Add the wine, tangerine juice and broth and reduce the liquid by half, about 8–10 minutes. In a blender whirl the sauce until smooth.

Return the sauce to the pan and add ¼ cup of the reserved coconut milk. Salt and pepper to taste.

To serve, plate the chicken breasts and top with the sauce.

I have included simple desserts that will please the sweet tooth and make a perfect ending to a wonderful meal. I have chosen recipes that are *gluten-free* and *refined sugar-free*. They are all very special and satisfyingly full of flavor.

Coconut Avocado Ice Cream

Makes over 1 quart

> 3 ripe medium avocados, chilled
> ¼ *scant* cup raw honey (taste mixture for desired sweetness)
> 2 cans (13.5 ounces coconut milk), chilled
> juice of 2–3 limes

Peel and pit the avocados and place the flesh into a food processor. Add the honey, lime juice, and chilled coconut milk and whirl to blend. Pour the mixture into an ice cream maker and freeze according to manufacturer's directions. Pour the mixture into the metal container (which has been in the freezer) and freeze until firm, about 2 hours.

Berry Blissful Ice Cream

Makes over 2 quarts

This ice cream made from coconut milk has all the richness of real cream. I promise.

> **4 cans coconut milk**
> **½** *scant* **cup raw honey (taste mixture for desired sweetness)**
> **You can use Stevita packets or drops for the sweetener instead of the honey**
> **1 pound of your favorite berries, strawberries, raspberries or blueberries**
> **1 teaspoon vanilla (optional)**

In a blender or food processor, puree the berries, coconut milk and honey until very well blended. Refrigerate until the mixture is very cold or put it in the freezer to chill rapidly.

Using your home electric ice cream machine, process the ice cream according to the manufacturer's directions. Eat immediately if not sooner.

To store the ice cream, transfer to a plastic container with a lid and place in the freezer. You may have to soften it in the refrigerator before serving the next time.

Lemon Curd or Lime Curd Tart with Nut Crust

Serves 8

You won't believe how good this tart is. And you can use the curd for other desserts too. Try layering it in a wide mouthed wine glass with the Fresh Raspberry Sauce and whipped cream.

> ½ cup lemon or lime juice
> 1 tablespoon zest
> ½ cup honey
> 6 egg yolks beaten
> 1 tablespoon *non-GMO* corn starch mixed with 1 tablespoon water
> ½ cup (one stick) KerryGold butter cut in tiny pieces

Garnish: Sweetened whipped cream, sprigs of fresh mint

Beat the egg yolks until pale in color and then put them through a sieve into a small saucepan.

Add the honey, lemon juice and the corn starch mixture to the pan. Cook over medium heat whisking constantly until the lemon mixture begins to boil and becomes thick, Remove from heat immediately and strain into a small bowl. Whisk in the butter pieces and the zest. This is enough curd for a 9" tart. Pour the curd into your pre-baked tart shell. Refrigerate until the curd is set.

To serve, garnish the tart with a little dollop of whipped cream and the sprigs of mint.

You might as well make a double batch while you're at it. The curd makes a welcome Christmas gift in a small jar with a pretty ribbon.

Nut Crust:
> 2¼ cups pecans or walnuts
> 3 ounces Medjool dates

¼ teaspoon vanilla

⅛ teaspoon salt

In the food processor, whirl the nuts with the dates, vanilla and salt until finely ground. Add a tablespoon of water if necessary to moisten the mixture. Pat the crust into a 9 inch fluted tart pan and bake at 350 for about ten minutes until the crust is slightly browned. Watch carefully so it does not burn.

Meyer Lemon Panna Cotta with Blackberries

Serves 6

Panna Cotta is comfort food supreme. This version is very lemony.

> 1 packet unflavored gelatin
> ¼ cup plus 2 tablespoons cold water
> ¼ scant cup raw honey or stevia to taste
> 2 cups heavy cream
> 2 tablespoons fresh Meyer lemon juice or (½ lemon & ½ orange juice)
> 2 tablespoons grated lemon rind

Garnish: Blackberries, raspberries or blueberries and lemon zest

In a small bowl, sprinkle the gelatin over 3 tablespoons of water in a small bowl. Let sit until softened, about 5 minutes.

In a medium saucepan, combine honey, lemon juice and rind and heavy cream; bring to a boil over medium heat. Remove from heat and whisk in the gelatin.

Divide the mixture into 6 straight sided bar glasses. Cover the glasses with plastic wrap and refrigerate for 5–6 hours. Serve chilled with berries and lemon zest.

Coconut Milk Panna Cotta with Fresh Raspberry Sauce

Serves 8–10

Unbelievably silky in texture! You will swoon.

1½ envelopes of unflavored gelatin
16 ounces coconut milk
¼ "scant" cup raw honey
1 teaspoon vanilla
2 cups heavy cream
Pinch sea salt

In a small bowl, sprinkle gelatin over ¼ cup cold water and set aside to soften.

Set out 8 straight sided bar glasses.

In a saucepan bring the coconut milk and honey to a boil. Remove from heat and add vanilla. Let the mixture cool to 130 degrees, then add the gelatin and stir to make sure the gelatin is dissolved. Slowly whisk in the heavy cream.

Pour the warm cream mixture into wide bar glasses and cover with saran wrap. Refrigerate the panna cotta for 5–6 hours.

To serve, cap each of the panna cottas with some of the Raspberry Sauce and garnish with more fresh raspberries and a sprig of mint.

Fresh Raspberry Sauce
4 cups fresh or frozen organic raspberries
1 tablespoon raw honey or 2 packets Stevita (to taste)
1 tablespoon fresh lemon juice

Place the ingredients in the food processor and process until liquefied. Strain the mixture through a sieve. This sauce is fresh and bright. It is best to use the same day you make it. Freeze leftover sauce for smoothies.

Lemon-Lime Coeur a la Crème with Fresh Raspberry Sauce

Serves 6

This dessert is impressive if you make it in the traditional coeur a la crème ramekins that have holes in the bottom. You can buy these at a good kitchen store. Buy the individual ramekins, about 4 ounces each, or one large one.

4 ounces organic cream cheese
¼ cup cottage cheese
¼ cup sour cream
½ cup heavy cream
1 tablespoon fresh lemon juice
1 tablespoon fresh lime juice
1 teaspoon each lemon and lime zest
2 packets Stevita
Pinch sea salt

Line each ramekin with a double piece of cheesecloth cut to overlap the sides. In the food processor, combine the cream cheese, cottage cheese, sour cream, lemon & lime juices, and zests. Blend until smooth scraping sides as needed. Remove the mixture to a bowl.

In a separate bowl whip the heavy cream and pinch of salt with an electric beater or a whisk until stiff peaks form. Add the whipped cream to the cheese mixture, in three separate additions folding well each time.

Divide the mixture into the lined ramekins. Place the ramekins on a sheetpan and cover loosely with plastic wrap. Some liquid will come out the holes onto the sheetpan. Let refrigerate 24 hours or until well set.

To serve invert the Coeur a la Crèmes onto dessert plates. Serve with the Fresh Raspberry Sauce and a sprig of mint.

Raspberry Gratin

Serves 6

Raspberries are my favorite berry. Raspberries baked in a custard make this dessert a superb combination. In this recipe, instead of using milk, I use heavy cream. Peaches or nectarines would work for this dessert as well. You can get everything ready before dinner and then it just takes minutes to finish when you are ready for dessert.

> ¾ cups heavy cream
> ¾ cups water
> 3 extra large egg yolks, whisked
> ¼ cup raw honey
> 2 tablespoons, non-GMO corn starch
> 2 tablespoons KerryGold butter, cut into small pieces
> pinch of sea salt
> 1 cup organic crème fraiche or sour cream
> 1 pint raspberries
> 1 tablespoon organic brown sugar (so the top browns)

In a heavy bottomed saucepan, bring the heavy cream and water to a boil and then immediately turn off the heat. Whisk the egg yolks in a medium bowl with the honey and the corn starch. Continue whisking until the yolks are a pale lemon color. Slowly whisk in the hot cream mixture, a few tablespoons at a time at first and then add the rest of the cream.

Return the egg/cream mixture to the stove in the same saucepan and cook over medium heat until the pastry cream thickens to a pudding-like consistency. Remove from the stove and add the butter and salt. Place the mixture in a bowl, covered with plastic and refrigerate until cool. Then fold in the crème fraiche.

To finish the gratin, preheat the broiler.

Scatter half the raspberries on the bottom of an attractive gratin dish (9 x 9 inches) or a round glass pie pan. Spoon the custard over the top of the raspberries. Scatter the remaining berries on top. Sprinkle the top of the gratin with the sugar and broil the dessert for 5–7 minutes until nice and brown and bubbling.

Serve immediately!

Earl Grey Pots de Crème

Serves 4

A very taste-full and elegant dessert!

> 1½ ounces Trader Joe's organic 73% Dark Chocolate Bar, chopped
> 1 cup organic whipping cream
> ⅔ cup water
> 3 Earl Grey tea bags
> 4 egg yolks
> 1 packet stevia or Stevita drops to taste (optional) taste mixture for desired sweetness

Garnish: ½ cup whipped cream, sweetened with a little stevia (optional) and a ¼ teaspoon vanilla. Grated chocolate bar.

Preheat oven to 325 degrees. Set out 4–6 ounce ramekins.

Place the chopped chocolate in a small bowl. In a small saucepan heat the cream and water to boiling. Pour ½ cup of the hot cream over the chocolate and stir. Whisk the chocolate until smooth. Add the teabags to the remaining cream in the saucepan and let steep for 10–12 minutes.

In another bowl whisk the eggs until lemon colored; add the warm cream mixture and then the melted chocolate cream and whisk again until the mixture is well blended.

Divide the mixture into the 4 ramekins. Place the ramekins in a rectangular glass baking dish and pour boiling water into the dish until the water comes halfway up the sides.

Cover the pan with foil and bake for 30–35 minutes until the custards are just set. Remove from oven, remove foil and let stand for 15 minutes. Cover each cup with plastic wrap and refrigerate 4 hours.

Serve with a dollop of the whipped cream. Grate some more chocolate bar on top.

Meyer Lemon Scented Ricotta Cream

Serves 4–5

This is a very simple, elegant dessert.

> **One 15 ounce container organic whole milk ricotta**
> **4 tablespoons Meyer lemon juice or regular lemons (½ lemon &**
> **½ orange juice is nice)**
> **2 packets Stevita or 1 tablespoon raw honey**
> **1 tablespoon lemon or orange zest**
> **½ cup toasted almonds**

Garnish: 1 pint organic berries, dark chocolate bar, grated

Using a large sieve lined with cheesecloth place the ricotta in the sieve over a bowl and refrigerate overnight. Pull some of the cheesecloth over the top of the ricotta to cover and place a weight on top so the liquid drains into the bowl underneath.

In a bowl, beat the ricotta until smooth and fluffy. Stir in the remaining ingredients evenly. Chill. To serve, spoon into wide mouthed wine glasses. Using a carrot peeler, grate the chocolate bar on top of the dessert for garnish. For a holiday variation omit the lemon and add brandy or another favorite liquor.

I Am Awakening Key Lime Pie

Makes one 9-inch pie

This cloud light pie comes via the generosity of Terces Engelhart and her pastry chef Tizana Alipo Tamborra at Café Gratitude in Berkeley, California. This recipe comes from her new book, *Sweet Gratitude*.

For the Crust:
- 1¼ cups macadamia nuts
- 1¼ cups pecans
- 3 ounces date paste or blended Medjool dates (blend in food processor with a few drops of water)
- ¼ teaspoon vanilla
- ⅛ teaspoon salt

For the Filling:
- ¾ cup lime juice
- 6 tablespoons agave syrup
- 1 cup mashed avocado
- ¼ cup plus coconut milk
- 2 teaspoons vanilla
- ⅛ teaspoon salt
- 3 tablespoons lecithin
- ¾ cup coconut oil (melted over a warm water bath)

Garnish: 1 lime, thinly sliced

To Make the Crust

In the bowl of your food processor fitted with the "S" blade, process pecans, macadamia nuts, vanilla, and salt until small and crumbly. Continue processing while adding small amounts of the chopped dates until the crust sticks together. Press crust into greased (with raw unscented coconut butter) 9-inch pie pan.

To Make The Filling

Blend all ingredients except the lecithin and coconut butter until smooth. Add lecithin and melted coconut oil, blending until well incorporated. Pour into prepared crust and set in fridge/freezer (for about an hour) until firm. Once set, spread a thin layer of meringue on top and decorate with lime slices.

I Am The Top Live Coconut Meringue:

Yields 2 ½ cups

> ¾ ounce Irish Moss*
> ½ cup water
> 1 cup coconut milk
> ½ cup fresh coconut meat
> ½ cup soaked raw cashews (soaked in water for 12 hours)*
> 5 tablespoons agave nectar
> 1 teaspoon lemon juice
> 1 tablespoon vanilla
> ⅛ teaspoon salt
> 1½ teaspoons lecithin
> ½ cup melted coconut butter

Blend Irish moss and water until smooth and thick. Add coconut milk, meat, cashews, agave, lemon juice, vanilla and salt. Blend until smooth. Add lecithin and melted coconut oil until well incorporated. Pour into a wide, shallow pan and set in fridge for up to 3 hours or overnight. When set, top pie; and if you like, peak with the back of a spoon.

*Irish Moss is a seaweed currently harvested off the coast of Jamaica. It is used to thicken and bind desserts and cheeses. Rinse Irish moss well in cool water and soak 12–24 hours before using in recipe.

*After soaking the cashews, rinse and drain.

Nora's Coconut Bliss Truffles

Makes a lot!

I adapted Nora Gedgaudas' recipe for these delicious, truffle-like morsels. Since I have always craved cookies and candy, these are the perfect solution to what to eat instead. I have tried them out on all my friends and they agree, they are richly satisfying and fill the bill when the sweet tooth needs soothing. Now I eat these instead of a cookie when I get carbohydrate cravings. Just to let you know the truffles, once they are made, have to be kept in the refrigerator. Toasting the nuts and coconut makes a huge difference in the flavor.

> 2 cups almond butter
> 8 ounces "Artisana" Raw Organic Coconut Butter (fabulous) or 8 ounces Artisana Cacao Bliss* or 8 ounces KerryGold butter if you want to minimize the coconut flavor
> 1 cup Bob's Red Mill coconut flour or 1 cup organic cocoa powder for the chocolate version*
> 1 cup sesame-flax mix (equal parts ground sesame and flax seeds)
> 2 cups *toasted* almonds, pecans or pistachios (soak nuts overnight first, then rinse)
> 1 cup organic dried coconut, *lightly* toasted
> 1 tablespoon vanilla
> 1 packet Stevita (optional)
> ½ teaspoon sea salt, use your own taste on the salt

Grind the toasted nuts very fine in the food processor.

In the food processor whirl the almond butter and the coconut butter together. Blend in the coconut flour. Transfer the mixture to a large bowl and mix in the remaining ingredients. Blend thoroughly.

Spoon the mixture out in teaspoon size amounts the size of a small walnut. They do not have to be completely round as truffles are sort of misshapen anyway. Roll the truffles in organic unsweetened cocoa powder, toasted coconut or more of the finely ground nuts (try macadamia nuts).

This recipe will make a lot of truffles. You can serve them at your next party (in little paper candy cups) or freeze them and thaw when the mood strikes. The mood strikes me about three times a day and I don't leave the house without a truffle.

*For the chocolate version of the truffles there is a chocolate Artisana Cacao Bliss *www.premierorganics.org*

*Try Holy Kakao or Dagoba organic cocoa powder.

Baked Figs with Lavender and Almonds

Serves 6

Figs speak of summer.

> 18 large ripe summer figs
> ¾ cup toasted almonds, chopped fine
> ¼ cup raw honey
> 8 tablespoons port
> a couple of lavender flowers (the lavender flowers must be organic)

In a small saucepan, cook the honey, lavender, port and 1 tablespoon water until a thick syrup. Strain lavender from syrup.

Preheat the oven to 350.

Cut the figs in half and place cut side down in a large rectangular glass baking pan. Bake 20 minutes. Then turn the figs cut side up and baste with the syrup. Bake 5 more minutes.

To serve, place 6 fig halves figs on each dessert plate. Pour remaining sauce over the figs and sprinkle with the chopped almonds. Garnish with additional lavender flowers. To dress up this dessert serve the figs with vanilla coconut milk ice cream.

Mediterranean Orange Almond Cake

Serves 8

This *flourless* cake is very moist and dense. It's perfect with tea. The eggs and almonds make this a high protein cake. It would also make a good breakfast or snack cake. Serve with whipped cream and raspberries for garnish.

> 2 organic Navel oranges
> 6 eggs
> 2½ cups very finely ground almonds (you can use leftover almond meal from making almond milk)
> ½ cup raw honey
> 1 teaspoon baking powder
> pinch sea salt

Preheat the oven to 350.

Prepare a 9" springform pan with spray vegetable oil and a dusting of flour.

Wash the oranges then place them in a saucepan and cover with water. Boil gently 45 minutes to an hour with the cover on. Oranges should be very soft when done. Drain the oranges and cool.

Cut the oranges into large pieces and remove any seeds. Place the pieces in the food processor and grind until very fine. With the electric mixer, beat the eggs until light and frothy. Fold in the dry ingredients with a rubber spatula and mix well. Then fold in the oranges and mix well.

Pour the batter into the prepared pan and bake cake for about one hour. Remove from oven and cool on a rack.

Vanilla Pudding with Nuts

Serves 4

Your children will love this simple *sugarless* heartwarming dessert. I think it would be good for breakfast.

> **2 cups almond milk**
> **1–2 packets Stevita**
> **2 tablespoons organic, *non-GMO*, cornstarch**
> **pinch sea salt**
> **1 large egg, beaten**
> **1 teaspoon vanilla**

Garnish: 3 tablespoons chopped toasted nuts (almonds, pecans, or pine nuts) and cinnamon or grated nutmeg (optional)

In a saucepan over medium heat, combine ½ cup milk, stevia and cornstarch and whisk until well blended. Add remaining milk and salt and cook over medium low heat, stirring frequently, about 9 minutes.

Place the egg in a small bowl and add some of the hot milk mixture a couple of tablespoons at a time until the egg and milk are mixed well. Return the egg and milk mixture to the rest of the hot milk and whisk over low heat another three minutes. Remove from heat and stir in the vanilla.

Pour the pudding into a glass bowl and cover with saran wrap until ready to serve. Divide the pudding into 4 bowls and top each bowl with some of the toasted nuts and cinnamon.

I Am Lovely Fruit Cobbler

Makes one 10 x 12 inch pan of cobbler

Café Gratitude, in Berkeley California, is one of the most creative and healthy restaurants I have ever been in. I pay homage to Terces Engelhart, its founder, for her love and dedication to health and beautiful food. If you have never tried raw food recipes then you are in for a treat. I selected this dessert as a simple, but delicious taste adventure. I highly recommend you get the *I Am Grateful* cookbook and the new *Sweet Gratitude* cookbook collaborated with pastry chef Tizana Alipo Tamborra, and dive right in. All the recipes have magical names that your children will love and the books will encourage them to appreciate natural flavors.

For the crust:
> 4½ cups pecans or walnuts
> 3 ounces date paste or blended Medjool dates
> 2 tablespoons cinnamon
> 1 tablespoon vanilla
> ⅛ teaspoon salt

For the filling:
> 10 cups of your favorite sliced fruit, apples, pears, nectarines, white peaches, mangoes or berries
> 2 tablespoons lemon juice
> 1½ tablespoons agave syrup (optional)
> 1 tablespoon vanilla
> 1 teaspoon cinnamon
> ⅛ teaspoon salt

Process all the ingredients for the crust until the nuts are slightly chunky. Once ready, divide the crust ingredients into two equal portions. Sprinkle one portion evenly over the bottom of the pan and compact with a fork. Reserve the other portion for the topping.

For the filling, combine all the ingredients in a large bowl and mix well. Evenly distribute the filling on top of the crust. Then crumble the remaining portion of crust on the top.

The cobbler is best served on the day you make it.

Berries with Toasted Coconut Sauce

Serves 4

This is a sustainably delicious, guilt free, dessert.

> 4 cups sliced organic strawberries, raspberries or blueberries
> ½ cup plus 4 tablespoons shredded organic coconut (unsweetened)
> 1 can coconut milk
> 2 packets stevia
> 2 tablespoons heavy cream
> 1 teaspoon vanilla

Preheat the oven to 350 degrees.

Place the coconut on a sheetpan and toast in the oven until light brown, about 5 minutes. Watch carefully!

In a bowl whisk the coconut milk, stevia, cream and vanilla, until well incorporated. Stir in ½ cup toasted coconut, reserving the extra 4 tablespoons. You can chill the sauce or serve it at room temperature.

To serve, spoon a little of the sauce on the bottom of 4 wide mouth red wine glasses and then divide the berries into the glasses. Top the berries with the remaining coconut sauce. Sprinkle the remaining toasted coconut on top of each dessert.

Ripe Figs with Goat Cheese and Honey

Serves 4

Figs are a late summer delicacy not to be missed. I had two fig trees at my home in Napa. One was the familiar dark purple with a pink center and the other was light green with a pink center. I would go out and eat a breakfast of figs in the morning standing under the tree.

> **8 ripe figs**
> **3 tablespoons finely chopped, toasted walnuts**
> **½ cup soft goat cheese**
> **1 tablespoon mint leaves, slivered**
> **8 tablespoons raw organic honey**
> **1 tablespoon late harvest Gewürztraminer or Riesling**

In a small bowl mix the cheese, 2 tablespoons of the walnuts and the mint. In another bowl mix the honey and the wine.

After cutting the stems off the figs, make 2 vertical cuts in an X in each fig, only going ⅔ of the way down. Open each fig carefully to create a cavity in the center. Using a teaspoon, place a small amount of the cheese mixture in each fig and press the tops together.

If you are not going to serve the figs immediately, cover with saran wrap and refrigerate. To serve, place two figs each on dessert plates. Drizzle the honey/wine mixture and garnish with the remaining toasted walnuts and a sprig of mint.

Chimayo Chocolate Pots

Serves 6

A spicy Mexican version of Chocolate Pots de Crème. I would use this dessert for the holidays or as the sweet ending to a special dinner.

> 4 ounces organic, unsalted butter
> 10 ounces organic 73% organic dark chocolate, chopped
> 1 tablespoon espresso or really strong coffee
> 4 eggs separated
> ⅛ teaspoon cream of tartar
> 2 tablespoons raw honey
> 1 teaspoon vanilla
> ⅛ teaspoon Chimayo chile powder (optional)
> ⅛ teaspoon cinnamon
> Whipped cream (optional)

Melt the butter and chocolate together in a bowl placed over hot, boiling water. Whisk the egg yolks and espresso to the melted chocolate. Beat the egg whites with the cream of tartar until stiff, and then fold in the honey.

Fold ¼ of the beaten egg whites into the chocolate mixture and incorporate well. Fold in the remaining whites and mix well.

Divide into wide mouthed wine goblets, or six ounce white French ramekins. Refrigerate at least four hours. Dress up with a little whipped cream.

Nectarines and Blueberries with Balsamic Vinegar

Serves 6

Balsamic Vinegar and fruit make an unusual and interesting dessert.

2 tablespoons balsamic vinegar
1 packet Stevita or to taste
1 pound organic blueberries, about 3 cups
1 pound ripe organic nectarines or strawberries, sliced
twist of fresh pepper

In a small saucepan bring to a boil 1 cup of the blueberries, the balsamic vinegar and 1 packet stevia. Cook for 1 minute.

In a large bowl combine the remaining 2 cups of blueberries and the sliced nectarines. Toss the fruit in the hot blueberry syrup and the twist of black pepper. Let stand, stirring occasionally until ready to serve.

Serve in wide mouth red wine glasses.

Pears Stuffed with Cream Cheese

Serves 2

For this recipe use only organic cream cheese with *no vegetable gum.*

2 ripe pears (Bartlett) or another favorite pear, in season
½ lemon
6 tablespoons organic cream cheese or ricotta
2 tablespoons raw honey
Organic cocoa powder

Peel the pears and cut in half, lengthwise. Remove the core with a spoon. Rub the surface of the halves with the lemon to prevent discoloration. In a bowl, whip the honey and the cream cheese. You can add a couple drops of lemon juice if you like. Spoon the cheese mixture into the hollow part of the pear halves. Place the two halves on two dessert plates and dust with cocoa powder.

San Joaquin Cantaloupe Ice

Serves 6

I grew up in the Cantaloupe capital of the world, Coalinga and Huron, California. When the melons were too ripe to ship we could buy a crate of sweet vine ripened cantaloupe for one dollar. For this recipe find the sweetest late summer melon you can find. Coalinga, by the way, is also the Horned Toad capital of the world.

> **3 pounds ripe sweet cantaloupe**
> **2 packets Stevita or to taste**
> **1 tablespoon fresh squeezed lime juice**
> **1 teaspoon** *microplaned* **lime zest**
> **2 tablespoons toasted, unsalted pistachios, chopped**

Garnish: Shaved chocolate bar (Trader Joe's 73% organic dark bar would be great)

Cut the rind off the melon, cut the melon in half and remove the seeds. Cut the melon into chunks and puree the flesh in the food processor until liquefied. Add the stevia, lime juice and zest and blend briefly to incorporate. Freeze the mixture in an ice cream maker according to the manufacturer's directions.

To serve divide the cantaloupe ice into wide mouthed wine goblets. Sprinkle on the pistachios and using a carrot peeler, shave the chocolate on top.

Strawberries with Sparkling Grape Juice

Serves 6

What could be lighter and more refreshing?

> 1 pound organic strawberries, sliced
> 1 cup organic sparkling grape juice, or Asti Spumante
> 2 teaspoons fresh tarragon, leaves chopped (optional)
> pinch sea salt
> 1 Stevita packet (optional)
> ¾ cup thick Greek yogurt or crème fraiche
> 1 teaspoon vanilla

In a bowl toss the strawberries with the grape juice, salt, tarragon and stevia. Cover the bowl and let chill for one hour.

In a blender puree the mixture until smooth. Set one cup of the mixture aside. In a bowl blend the remaining mixture with the yogurt and vanilla. Taste for sweetness.

To serve put the yogurt/puree mixture in six wide mouth wine glasses. Drizzle a little of the reserved one cup of strawberry puree on top of each dessert.

Lovely Lotion for the Cook's Hands

1 cup olive oil
3 tablespoons coconut oil
3 tablespoons cocoa butter
1 ounce beeswax, available at the health food store or Whole Foods
¾ cup lavender water, or lemon verbena water
20 drops essential lavender or lemon oil*

In a saucepan over low heat, melt the olive oil, coconut oil, cocoa butter and beeswax together. Immediately remove from heat. When the oils are cool, put the mixture in a blender. While the blender is running add the scented water and the essential oil of your choice. The lotion will keep for six months, if it lasts that long.

The lotion makes a wonderful gift!

Please visit the Elizabeth Van Buren Web site for a wonderful selection of therapeutic grade essential oils and other products. *www. elizabethvanburen.com*

Resources

Sea Salt

San Francisco Bath Salt Company: *www.sfbsc.com* (great company for luxury bath salts, too)

Tropical Traditions: *www.tropicaltraditions.com*

Redmond RealSalt: *www.realsalt.com*

Whole Foods

Vitamin Supplements

Klaire Labs: *www.klair.com*

Dr. Ron's Ultra Pure: *www.Dr.Rons.com*

Herb Pharm, Liquid Herbal Extracts: *www.herbpharm.com*

Mercola: *www.mercola.com*

Sun Chlorella: *www.sunchorellausa.com*

Rockwell Nutrition: *www.rockwellnutrition.com*

Radiant Life Catalogue: *http://radianlifecatalogue.com*

Spices

Spice Hunter: *www.spicehunter.com*

Organic Planet: *www.organic-planet.com*

Rapunzel Pure Organics: *www.rapunzel.com*

Frontier Natural Products Co-Op: *www.frontiernaturalbrands.com*

Organic Oils

Bariani Organic Olive Oil: *www.barianioliveoil.com*

Long Meadow Ranch, Napa Valley, Organic Olive Oils: *www.longmeadowranch.com*

Barlean's Organic Oils: *www.barleans.com*

Spectrum Organics: *www.spectrumorganics.com*

California Estate Olive Oil and Market: *www.caloliveoil.com*

Stonehouse Olive Oil and Balsamic Vinegar:
  www.stonehouseoliveoil.com/products
Aunt Patty's Organic Extra Virgin Coconut Oil: *www.AuntPattys.com*
Gold Label Virgin Coconut Oil from the Philippines:
  www.tropicaltraditions.com
Omega Nutrition: *www.omeganutrition.com*
Organic Sesame Oil: *www.edenfoods.com*
www.chefshop.com

Dried Fruits & Nuts

Organic Planet: *www.organic-planet.com*
Braga Organic Farms: *www.buyorganics.com*
D&S Ranches: *www.california-almonds.com*
Organic Pastures, raw almonds: *www.organicpastures.com*
Morningside Farm: *www.morningsidefarm.com*
Living Tree Organics: *www.deliciousorganics.com*

Chocolate

Raw Organic Cocoa Powder, Sunfood: *www.sunfood.com*
Kokoa: 100% certified organic cocoa from the Dominican Republic
  and Bolivia
Chocolate Bars, Tropical Traditions: *www.tropicaltraditions.com*
Holykakow, righteous Organic Chocolate Syrups and Powders:
  www.holykakow.com

Nut Butters

World Pantry: *www.worldpantry.com*
Once Again Nut Butter: *www.onceagainnutbutter.com*

Organic Bulk Foods

Look for a source in your state
Azure Foods in Oregon: *www.azurestandard.com*

Organic Grains, Cereals, Seeds and Flours

Bob's Red Mill: *www.bob'sredmill.com*

Organic Planet: *www.organic-planet.com*

Arrowhead Mills: *www.arrowheadmills.com*

Eden Organics: *www.edenfoods.com*

Shiloh Farms: *www.shilofarms.com*

Lundberg Farms: *www.lundberg.com*

Tropical Traditions: *www.tropicaltraditions.com*

Fair Trade Rice: *www.altereco.com*

Organic Flavored Extracts and Syrups

Flavorganics: *www.flavorganics.com*

Environmentally Responsible Seafood Sources and Information

Ecofish, Inc: *www.ecofish.com*

Crown Prince Natural: *www.crownprince.com*

Vital Choice Seafood: *www.vitalchoice.com*

Blue Ocean Institute: *www3.blueocean.org*

Wild Oregon, Ocean-Line Caught Call Robin 503-591-7795

Monterey Bay Aquarium

Grass-Fed Meats and meats raised on sustainable ranches without hormones and antibiotics

American Grassfed Association: *www.americangrassfed.or/producers.htm*
www.greenpeople.org/OrganicMeathtml

Eat Wild: *www.eatwild.com* (look for the producers in your state)

Lonely Lane Farm, Oregon: *www.lonelylanefarms.com*

Long Meadow Ranch, Napa Valley, California: *www.longmeadowranch.com*

Niman Ranch: *www.nimanranch.com*

Eggs, Poultry and Dairy

Eat Wild: *www.eatwild.com*

Peaceful Pastures: *www.peacefulpastures.com*

Other Organic Web Sites

Community Supported Agriculture (CSA's): *www.csacenter.org*
www.theorganicpages.com
www.shopbyorganic.com
www.organic.com
www.efoodpantry.com
www.orgfood.com
www.sunorganic.com
www.greenforgood.com
www.organicfruits&nuts.com

Garden Seeds

Seed Savers Exchange: *www.seedsavers.org*
Seeds of Change: *www.seedsofchange.com*

Pure Water

Radiant Life 14-Stage Biocompatible Water Purifications System:
    www.radiantlifecatalogue.com
Brita Water Filters: *www.brita.com*
Reverse Osmosis Filters: *www.reverseosmosisfilters.net*
Filters Now: *www.filtersnow.com*
www.h@odistributors.com/index.asp

Organizations for further research:

Union of Concerned Scientists: *www.uscusa.org/food_and_agrictulture*
Weston A. Price Foundation: *www.westonprice.org*
Center For Informed Food Choices: *www.informedeating.org*
Eat Well: *www.eatwellguide.com*
Food Routes: *www.foodroutes.org*
The Pfeiffer Treatment Center, Nutritional Treatment for Mental Disorders:
    www.hriptc.com
The Soil Association: *www.soilassociation.com*
Seed Magazine, The Journal of Organic Living

Fair Trade Resource Network: *www.fairtraderesource.org*

Healthy Eating Politics: *www.healty-eating-politics.com*

Food Democracy Now: *www.fooddemocracynow.org*

Genetically Engineered Food Alert: *www.gefoodalert.org* or
    call 800-390-3373

The Future of Food DVD by Lily Films: *www.futureoffood.com*

Organization for World Food Supply Issues: *www.foodfirst.com*

Nutrition Brain: *www.nutritionbrain.com*

3 Steps to Conquering ADD-ADHD: *3stepsadd.com*

*Orthomolecular Health, for treatment of alcoholism, arthritis, high cholesterol, anxiety, weight loss, autism, crohn's disease, schizophrenia, Huntington's disease, learning disabilities, ADD, behavioral disorder, shingles (herpes) depression, HIV & AIDS, bi-polar disorder, asthma, multiple sclerosis. *www.Orthomolecularhealth.com*

*Orthomolecular.org

Recommended Books & Publications

Primal Body—Primal Mind: Empower your Total Health the Way Evolution Intended (. . . and Didn't), Nora T. Gedgaudas, CNS, CNT

The Schwarzbein Principle: The Truth About Losing Weight, Being Healthy, and Feeling Younger, Dr. Diana Schwarzbein

The UltraMind Solution, Mark Hyman, MD, *www.ultrawellness.com*

In Defense of Food and *The Omnivore's Dilemma,* Michael Pollan

Animal, Vegetable, Miracle, Barbara Kingsolver

The Wizard of the Upper Amazon: The Story of Manuel Cordova-Rios, F. Bruce Lamb

The Three Halves of Ino Moxo: Teachings of the Wizard of the Upper Amazon, César Calvo

I Am Grateful, Terces Engelhart, with Orchid

Sweet Gratitude, Terces Engelhart, with Tizana Tambora Alipo

Wild Fermentation: The Flavor, Nutrition, and Craft of Live-Culture Foods, Sandor Ellix Katz

Keep Chickens: Tending Small Flocks in Cities, Suburbs, and Other Small Spaces, Barbara Kilarski

Rainwater Harvesting: Guiding Principles to Welcome Rain into Your Life And Landscape, Brad Lancaster

Gaia's Garden: A Guide to Home-Scale Permaculture, Toby Hemenway

The Backyard Beekeeper: An Absolute Beginner's Guide to Keeping Bees in Your Yard and Garden, Kim Flottum

Barnyard in Your Backyard: A Beginner's Guide to Raising Chickens, Ducks, Geese, Rabbits, Goats, Sheep, and Cows, Gail Damerow

SASTUN, *My Apprenticeship with a Maya Healer*, Rosita Arvigo

The Hundred-Year Lie: How to Protect Yourself from the Chemicals that Are Destroying Your Health, Randal Fitzgerald

The End of Food: How the Food Industry is Destroying Our Food Supply and What We Can Do About It, Thomas F. Pawlick

Nutrition and Physical Degeneration, Weston Price, DDS

Nourishing Traditions: The Cookbook that Challenges Politically Correct Nutrition And the Diet Dictocrats, Sally Fallon

Eat Fat, Lose Fat, Sally Fallon and Mary Enig

The Queen of Fats: Why Omega-3's Were Removed from the Western Diet and What We Can Do to Replace Them, Susan Allport

Seeds Of Deception: Exposing Industry and Government Lies About the Safety of the Genetically Engineered Foods You are Eating, Jeffrey Smith

Nutrition and Mental Illness, Carl C. Pheiffer, MD, PhD

Nutritional Influences on Mental Illness: A Sourcebook of Clinical Research, Melvyn Werbach, MD

Anxiety: Orthomolecular Diagnosis and Treatment, Jonathan Prousky

Orthomolecular Medicine for Everyone, Abram Hoffer, MD, Phd and Andrew Saul, PhD

Smart Nutrients: Prevent and Treat Alzheimer's, Enhance Brain Function, Abram Hoffer MD, Phd, and Morton Walker

Treating Schizophrenia: Complimentary Vitamin & Drug Treatments, Abram Hoffer, MD, PhD

Index